TES

"Roxanne has taken a lifetime of leadership experience, the highs and lows, and wrapped it up as a gift to us in "Never Wear Red." Roxanne is a passionate, caring and inspiring leader who is also grounded in the practical realities of life and business. Roxanne is someone who practices what she preaches—she's the real deal!"

Jeanne Coughlin, President The Coughlin Group, Inc.

"Roxanne is a passionate leader and educator! She has enabled me to break through my own "glass ceiling", helping me to realize that I was standing in my own way of achieving my goals both professionally and personally. She is an engaging speaker and a force to be reckoned with. She will NOT allow you to fail or make excuses. I am so glad she has put her teachings on paper and has written such a powerful and motivating book. I now feel that Roxanne will always be with me, coaching and guiding me through life's challenges and rewards!!! The world is better a place because of Roxanne Kaufman Elliott, and I am better for knowing her!!!"

Amy Relihan, LensCrafters®

"Never Wear Red isn't your typical leadership book. It's a life book. Roxanne brilliantly takes us on a journey of understanding, accepting and developing self - the core of authentic leadership. You'll want to read it again and again."

Raquel Eatmon, CEO Rising Media LLC

"This book is a must read for anyone searching for purpose in their lives and a way to connect to their life's calling. Roxanne's powerful stories from her own life experiences bring an authentic perspective to helping others on their journey to greater fulfillment."

Loree W. Connors, CPA, CFO and Treasurer
Vita-Mix Corporation

"Never Wear Red is a leadership love story. It is not only Roxanne's inspiring personal journey but also a how-to guide to inspire, ignite and impact yourself and the world by living out your purpose and passion."

Aneta Ardelian Kuzma, Mom, Wife, Leader, MBA
Learner, Intellection, Input, Connectedness, Achiever

"Roxanne is the kind of person who, when you look in her eyes, you immediately see that she has a story to tell. As she speaks you can easily feel her warmth, passion, her ability to connect, and most of all...her humanness. Mixed with her direct and honest truth-telling, this is the essence of good leadership. This book reads exactly as a conversation with her would, and I can't recommend it enough. It's a warm and fuzzy read just as much as it is a structured manual for how to get your life together. As she says in her book "genuine leadership is defined by heart, integrity, honesty, courage, compassion and those many intangible qualities of being and creating the most authentic leader that resides inside each one of us." Roxanne embodies this definition, and is an incredible asset to her profession."

Dr. Elizabeth Elliott, Naturopathic Physician

This is a leadership book ... and a love story. Roxanne's amazing marriage of original and sage leadership knowledge with profound analysis of the human spirit is inspiring and exciting. She masterfully weaves her story into a practical guide which stirs the reader's soul to action. Roxanne's masterpiece is an easy read and yet a tome of wisdom and encouragement. Indispensable quintessential insight!

Timothy Relihan, Pfizer Corporation

Never Wear Red

A Leadership Love Story

Roxanne Kaufman Elliott

Published by Motivational Press, Inc.
1777 Aurora Road
Melbourne, Florida, 32935
www.MotivationalPress.com

Copyright 2017 © by Roxanne Kaufman Elliott

All Rights Reserved

No part of this book may be reproduced or transmitted in any form by any means: graphic, electronic, or mechanical, including photocopying, recording, taping or by any information storage or retrieval system without permission, in writing, from the authors, except for the inclusion of brief quotations in a review, article, book, or academic paper. The authors and publisher of this book and the associated materials have used their best efforts in preparing this material. The authors and publisher make no representations or warranties with respect to accuracy, applicability, fitness or completeness of the contents of this material. They disclaim any warranties expressed or implied, merchantability, or fitness for any particular purpose. The authors and publisher shall in no event be held liable for any loss or other damages, including but not limited to special, incidental, consequential, or other damages. If you have any questions or concerns, the advice of a competent professional should be sought.

Manufactured in the United States of America.

ISBN: 978-1-62865-397-7

Contents

Dedication 11
Acknowledgments 13
Forward 15
Preface 18
Introduction 23

PART I - INSPIRE

Chapter 1
Never Wear Red 31
  Manifesting vision 33
  The Power of Vision 34
  Words 34

Chapter 2
0.2mg Gold 37
  Past, Present & Future 38
  You First. 42
  Values and Principles 43
  Purpose & Passion 48
  Dreams 51
  Focus 52

Chapter 3
Grit 56
  The Board Room 57
  Courage 59

Worthiness 64
The Glass Ceiling 66
Personal Brand 67

CHAPTER 4
CROSS THE RIVER AND BURN THE BOAT 74
Motivation & Conditioning. 75
Forgiveness 78
Negativity 80
Self-Confidence – It can make or break your success... 83
Affirmations 86

CHAPTER 5
PURPOSE. PASSION. POWER............................ 91
Define and Focus on Strengths 92
Employee Engagement in U.S. Stagnant in 2015............ 95
20 Million Dollars.. 97
The Black Line – or – Location, Location, Location 99
Personal Power Vs Authority 103

PART II - IGNITE

CHAPTER 6
REINVENT 114
The Formula..114
The Gang & The Nun 120

CHAPTER 7
LEADERSHIP & STRATEGY 127
What is Leadership and How Do I Get Some? 127
Are Leaders Born or Made? 129

    Strategy 131
    Your True North 132
    The Five Pointed Star – Organizing the Strategy 133
    Big Hairy Audacious Goals 136
    Mission & Critical Goal Categories 138
    WHYSMART Goals 139

CHAPTER 8
MEETING OLD FRIENDS FOR THE FIRST TIME 143
    Emotional Intelligence 146
    Motivation 151
    6 Components of Hidden Motivation 153
    Myths 154

CHAPTER 9
DON'T LOOK BACK – YOU ARE NOT GOING THAT WAY. 158
    A Cherokee Legend - Two Wolves 159
    Ghosts 160
    Discipline 162
    Focus 162

PART III - IMPACT

CHAPTER 10
DO OR DO NOT. THERE IS NO TRY. YODA 168
    Executing on the Plan 170
    The i3 Process 172
    Vision 173
    Critical Goal Categories 175
    Why Smart Goals 176
    Leadership Development Plan Summary 178

Chapter 11

The Secret Sauce 181
The Four-Letter Word 181
Empathy & Compassion 183

Chapter 12

Cornerstones 185
The Foundation 185
Value 186
Gold Nuggets 189
The Art of Changing Yourself 192
Blessings 193

Resources 197

Dedication

To my 'tribe'.

For my family and friends... each of you is a 'heart of gold'. Your love, support, understanding and friendship are what sustain and nurture me every day. I could not have written this love story without you... you are at the very heart of it. Each of you has taught me – and continues to teach me – the most important leadership lessons of my life and what genuine leadership is and is not.

Some of you encourage; some of you hold my feet to the fire; some of you criticize when I need it most (and like it the least); some of you make me laugh out loud and with abandon; and some of you make me pause and re-think what I know and don't know; and still others of you simply let me be who and what I am in any moment.

For all of this and all the rest – thank you. You make my life rich and full of adventures, moments and memories that are imprinted on my heart and soul forever.

> "What lies behind us and what lies before us are small matters compared to what lies within us. And when we bring what is within us out into the world, miracles happen."
>
> **Ralph Waldo Emerson**

Acknowledgments

As with any endeavor of major proportion, writing a book can be a daunting and somewhat overwhelming event. As I have worked on this "Never Wear Red" event over the past year, there have been many people who have been there along the way offering their love, support, encouragement, resources, time and effort.

To my Kaufman Elliott family, I thank you for your patience and understanding for all the times I have fallen off the radar, disappeared into my office for hours and days, forgotten to call you back and have been forgetful and distracted. You have been so patient and understanding – never complaining or criticizing – you are just always there. Special thanks to my beautiful sister, Amy, husband, Tim, my niece Molly and daughter Dane for being the first to read the beginning of the raw manuscript and giving me your honest feedback and encouragement.

To my husband, George – thank you for just letting me be me. For always having my back and for your endless patience and love. You are my 'steady as she goes' guidepost and foundation. You always bring me back down to earth when I start to drift too far, but never in a way that is limiting – always in a way that is loving. You are such a gift to me.

To my friend and colleague, Raquel Eatmon. I do not know how to thank you for your unconditional love, support and guidance. You inspire and challenge me... and make me laugh out loud! You have helped me enormously in sharing your experience and knowledge in writing and publishing this book and in dealing with the myriad of emotions, frustrations and challenges along the way. Thank you, dear friend.

Everyone needs BDAGs. Mine have been and continue to be invaluable in helping me to make this book a reality and in shaping many of my business decisions. BDAGs are Bold Daring Audacious Gals (or Guys). Mine are 'sisters' as well as BDAGs: Sharon Toerek, Jeanne Coughlin and Kelly Ferrell. We formed our accountability group four years-ago. Throughout this time, we have met for three hours each month (with only one missing one month) to report out on our businesses and lives. We do not judge or criticize – we ask a lot of questions and hold each accountable to our goals and plans. This is a group of amazing women. Each successful in her own business, and yet each dedicated to helping each other grow and develop. Thank you, my BDAGs. You held me to light the fire on this book!

To Daisy, my ever constant, devoted and loving companion. This little Beagle has been my confidante, always present friend and sounding board for my fears, triumphs, successes and failures. My heartfelt gratitude to Aneta Ardelian Kuzma, my dear friend and colleague, for writing such an amazing forward for this book and sharing so much of experience and wisdom with me over the years.

To Stacey Rodgers, Doreen Chester, Loree Connors, Darcy Zehe, all of my SOAR sisters, the old team on the East Coast, my friends at COSE, MFTBP and Leadership Lorain County, all of my kids, family and friends far and wide and across all the years – you are all part of this book. You have taught me and continue to teach me how to become the best version of myself. I am still working on it. Thank you with all of my heart.

Forward

For anyone who had a dream, who stopped dreaming, or who has been caught in the lies and limitations that this life offers, this book is for you. For those who aspire to imagine a new future, to discover their true selves and life's purpose – again, or for the first time - this book is for you. For those who have already decided to create, design, and imagine a better life starting today, this book is also for you.

Reading "Never Wear Red" is the next best thing to knowing Roxanne Kaufman Elliott. Her energy, wisdom, spunkiness and love for life emanates on every page. I have the privilege of calling Roxanne a friend, coach and mentor. When we met at a conference years ago I knew that we sat next to each other for a reason and that our lives would be connected. Roxanne radiates joy and love – from her red hair, to her smile and infectious laugh and her warm embraces.

When Roxanne asked me to write her forward, I was surprised, honored, humbled and frightened. I am not an author, nor am I a recognizable name. Why am I qualified to write the foreword to this amazing book? So instead I decided to approach this as an opportunity to introduce my dear friend to each of you. That I can do because Roxanne has been a personal inspiration to me. She has built a life living her true purpose based on her passion and authentic self. This book allows her to share that with everyone who reads it.

Roxanne's career spans over 25 years. She has worked in corporate America, as a consultant, entrepreneur, keynote speaker, executive coach, strategic planner, author and humanitarian. At her core, she is a lightning rod – a catalyst for change. Roxanne encourages us to dream BIG and without limitations. She paints a picture about how meaningful and impactful we can be in this world if we focus on our passion and purpose. She then places before us a path, a recipe, our modus operandi to begin our journey.

Many of us, like me, have struggled with writing a vision statement for our life. It's easier to help someone else identify what they're good at rather than hold the mirror up to ourselves. This book teaches us how to examine what we're already doing to imagine the best version of our future selves. Roxanne urges us to stop listening to the voices from the past that told us that we weren't good enough, that we couldn't do something or that we shouldn't do something we loved. Instead, embrace your uniqueness and that which makes you, you.

Did you know that every human being has 0.2 mg of gold in their body? I didn't, yet, Chapter 2 focuses on that "nugget of magic that we each possess". Roxanne reminds us that we're not limited by our past, or even our current situations. Instead, we are accountable for what we do with our talents and true change requires focus, effort and courage.

When I think about why my own journey has taken so long, I may have said that I didn't have time, that I was being responsible, that I was blessed and shouldn't complain about my circumstances. However, I never would have said that I was fearful or that I lacked courage. Roxanne challenges what I always believed courage to be. She states that courage is like leadership and we can learn it by practicing it often. Like the

Cowardly Lion, we must face our fears daily and in spite of them, do that which causes us fear until it no longer has a hold on our lives.

There are many leadership books on the market. This one is unique, and authentically a reflection of its author and her approach to life. Through Roxanne's personal stories she inspires us; through tools and a strategic plan tied to your core values she'll ignite that inspiration and finally propel you to positively impact the world around you. What stories do you need to un-tell yourself in order to find your authentic self? What is your 0.2 mg of gold – that unique combination of self, skill, experience, passion – your own personal brand - that is uniquely you? And, how will you use that to propel yourself to greatness to help others?

"Never Wear Red" is a leadership love story. It is not only Roxanne's inspiring personal journey but also a how-to guide to inspire, ignite and impact yourself and the world by living out your purpose and passion.

"To be what we are, and to become what we are capable of becoming, is the only end of life."
Baruch Spinoza

Aneta Ardelian Kuzma
Mom, Wife, Leader, MBA
Learner, Intellection, Input, Connectedness, Achiever

Preface

I believed I could fly.

I was inspired.

I believed I had super powers.

I could ignite my powers to create good in the world.

I believed... in magic...in possibilities... in me.

I created.

I dreamed.

I imagined.

I got caught.

I got caught flying, powering, dreaming, imagining... and was told... **TO STOP**.

Grow up.

Pay attention.

Get serious.

Stay inside the lines.

Do this.

Don't do that.

Be this.

"NEVER WEAR RED"

Don't be that.

Do as I say. Not as I do.

You cannot.

You should not.

You will not.

You are odd.

You are DIFFERENT.

Face the music.

Get real.

Get serious.

So I did... or at least tried. **They** were, after all, the "grown-ups", the "BIG brains", the

"Ones Who Know Stuff".

THE **OWKS**.

So I stopped...
Believing.
Flying.
Imagining.
Powering.
Being.
Me.

And became everything I was supposed to be and everything everyone expected me to be... sort of.

It didn't work.

30 years later, I was still trying to figure out how to be what they told me to be. And then I realized, I was living someone else's life by everyone else's expectations instead of the one person's that was the most important—mine.

And then, I said **"STOP."** I did. They did.

I wear **RED.**

I believe I can fly.

I believe I have super powers.

I dream. Big, bigger, bigger... and bigger.

I imagine. Beyond the universe and back and beyond again.

I believe... in magic... in possibilities... in me.

And in you.

Get up. Look in the mirror. Who are you? What is your purpose? What is your passion? Start answering these questions and you will be on your way to unleashing your inner Champion and your genuine power. You will Emerge as a Champion.

You will be YOU. Really. Genuinely. Authentically. You.

Do it.

It's hard.

NO, wait. It's not hard. It's really hard.

Do it anyway.

Wear Red.

Cross the river and burn the boat.

Stop wasting time. Stop being a victim. Commit to becoming YOU.

And as you do, remember... there is no "end point"—no "hoorah, I've reached Nirvana"—no "bravo" you are now "you"—

nope none of that. As the old adage goes—this is a journey not a destination. So be prepared—it's tough, hard, frustrating —but you are up to the task.

Show up. It does get better. It gets incredible. And the rewards are priceless. Finally becoming the best version of you.

Joy. Happiness. Success. Who knew?

This book shares a bit of my and other's philosophy, story, journey and lessons learned so far. It offers both practical and thought-provoking ways for you to find and unleash your own unique and limitless power and become your own best champion. Find your success and happiness on your terms, in your way and in your time.

It will always be a work in progress for anyone who takes up the challenge—but oh my, what a ride!

Here's the challenge—are you up to discovering who you truly are, where you are and where you are going? And more importantly, are you ready to determine if you like what you discover, or if, perhaps, you find some things you would like to change, add or eliminate? This is not a quick fix to anything. Regardless of what you may have been told—there is no silver bullet. A genuine life requires genuine work.

You have the capacity for success and happiness already within you. Unleash it!

So. Here's to you and your journey. I wish you abundant love and super power strength **to inspire, ignite and impact** your life, the lives of others, the world and the universe... to become what and who you are destined to become.

Wear Red. Be. Do. Become. You. Emerge as a champion.

Feel free to let me know how it goes for you.

Roxox

> "IT IS NEVER TOO LATE TO BECOME WHAT YOU MIGHT HAVE BEEN."
>
> **GEORGE ELIOT**

Introduction

This book is for and about you. Your life. Your success. Your happiness. You becoming your best you. And the only person who can make that happen is you.

Did you know that every human being has 0.2 mg of gold in their body? Every one of us. Most of this gold is within the heart. Having a "heart of gold" is more than just an old saying—it's actually true. How do we get to it? How do we use our gold—mine it out— and unleash it to become the leaders, the people, we are meant to be?

It's about...

Awareness. Awareness of the obstacles standing in our way of success. Awareness and understanding of our own worth and power. We have everything we need right now to become the person we've always wanted to be. Become aware of the "Never Wear Red" statements, attitudes, behaviors and influences in your life that have created barriers to your success and happiness (self-generated and those from others) and learn how to overcome them

Knowledge. Learning new skills and ways of thinking and approaching our lives and careers.

Attitude. Shifting away from self-defeating attitudes and myths that get in our way of digging out our gold.

Learning. Life-long learning—about ourselves, others and the world in which we live.

Belief. Believing in self. Believing in our own inner champion. Believing that we have the power to transform our lives; become the best version of ourselves; and create a life of happiness and success beyond our wildest imaginings.

And so much more...

This is not a psychology book. It is not a self-help book. It is a leadership book. Albeit, one of a different color, but a leadership book none the less. It is about getting out of your way: taking 100% responsibility for your life, and finding your success and happiness in your way and in your time.

You already have everything you need to make this happen. You just need to do it.

The only person in the world who can create your life, in your time and in your way—is you. And that "you" has to be your most authentic and genuine self, empowered by knowing and doing what only you can do best in the world. As you become more and more focused on the life and legacy you want to create and the person you want to become, you find clarity of purpose, renewed focus and energy and the motivation to re-invent to the next highest level of you.

Three words are the foundation of what I have learned and continue to learn about leadership of self and then leadership of others—**inspire, ignite and impact. It's about** passion, purpose— and inspiration. Ignite your inspiration with a solid strategic plan aligned to your core values and authentic self. Take the action necessary to make the impact you dream of—on your life and the lives of others. Do it on your terms, in your way and in your time.

Transformation and reinvention will be the result, and you will find your **"i to the power of 3"**. It's all about spending the time and effort to grow; learning through the failures and successes; and opening ourselves up to the world no matter how scary or intimidating. It's becoming real.

To **inspire** ourselves or anyone else, we must first know and understand ourselves at a deeper level than we ever have before. We need to uncover our true passion and talents. Once we find that, we become inspired and find that we can inspire others to do the same—with truth, passion, values, intention, purpose and consciousness.

It's a wonderful thing to have a vision of where you are going and to finally begin to understand who you are, what gifts and talents you possess and what excites and motivates you. But, if you don't have a plan to actualize this inner knowledge, it will stay where it is—internal! You must **ignite** your passion in order to grow, evolve and emerge as a champion!

Now you have your inspiration and plan to ignite it. Next final step? Make an **impact**—you must take action! Hour by hour, day by day, week by week, month by month and so on... you need to follow-up on your vision and your planning with specific goals and action. You need to do the work. And you will begin to see the life you have imagined—become real.

The 'i's are in lower case because they do not have room for ego. We must set aside our egos and just be truly who we are. I know what you're thinking, "but I do that already!" And good for you if you do, but I still challenge you to read on and see if you can raise that bar even higher.

The three 'i's' are the three keys to discovering and developing your inner leader and to emerge as a champion. If we are to become the very best human being we can in all aspects of our life on earth, then we need to understand and embrace our very own, unique and powerful 'i'.

It's how we learn to break down the barriers and obstacles... and **wear red.**

What will inspire you to learn? Let's find out.

PART I

INSPIRE

THERE IS AN OVERWHELMING need in our world, communities, societies, schools, neighborhoods, churches and businesses for real, genuine, authentic leadership. There is a leadership chasm in our world today—and one that continues to widen at an alarming pace—with alarming consequences.

The word 'leadership' as it is used often in these pages, is not the leadership most people think of when they hear the word. The leadership I speak of is not defined by title, position, authority, rank, money, education or any of the other typical descriptors applied to this word.

Genuine leadership is defined by heart, integrity, honesty, courage, compassion and those many intangible qualities of being and creating the most authentic leader that resides inside each one of us. Intangible as these things may seem on the outside, they hold the power of creating incredibly tangible results that impact our world, communities, societies, schools, neighborhoods, churches, businesses and our personal and professional growth, success, peace and happiness. And none of this kind of leadership power has anything to do with where you came from, title, position, authority, rank, money, education or any of the other typical descriptors. That power—that leadership power, comes from who you are—who you genuinely, authentically are and who you are meant to become. And we need you.

It all starts with inspiration.

To inspire ourselves or anyone else we must first know and understand ourselves at a deeper level than we ever have before. We need to uncover our true passion and talents—and our true leader. Once we find that, we become inspired and find that we can inspire others to the same. There is no room for ego in any of this – only truth, passion, values, intention, purpose and consciousness.

Leadership starts with self. It is first and foremost a relationship with yourself. We must know who we are and why before we can begin to truly lead ourselves or others. The journey begins with self-discovery and understanding—and finding that spark within you that lights up your purpose and your power. This is what **inspires** you in both the short and long term.

As you begin to learn more about yourself—where you excel and where you do not—you can look at the choices you have made so far in your life and have some real aha moments about why things went badly or why they went well! I am a firm believer in living in our strengths and whenever I can, finding someone else to cover the not-so-strong-stuff. This where we need a secret code ring or some other icon known only to us—to remind us of our strengths. Mine happen to be Red Shoes. But more on that later—yes, there is a story.

Just like your life (and probably everyone else's to some degree) thus far, this path will have its share of naysayers and bullies. They will start to show-up in some rather impressive numbers and with very compelling reasons why you should stop doing what you are doing. And when they do, there is a good chance you will react as you did when you were a kid or a teenager—and that's rarely a good thing. They will sling the sticks and stones whenever they can to make you STOP. Why? Maybe fear? Fear of the unknown? Because you are different? Because they perceive you as smarter, stronger and more successful? Remember, when someone tries to make less of you—it is all about them trying to make more of themselves. It's not about you. Remember the old rhyme, "sticks and stones may break my bones, but words will never hurt me!"

A funny thing happens when you start thinking about all of this and really discovering what inspires you. And you may be the last to see it—you begin to change in infinitesimal, but powerful, ways. Your mind opens to more possibilities and more opportunities; you begin to see your vision in more clarity than you have before, and you start to see what needs to happen for you to reach your goals and make that vision a reality. You become willing to cross the river and burn the boat.

The first step in becoming your most authentic self is to start asking the tough questions about who you are, where you have been, where you are now and where you are going and why? What are your non-negotiable values? Why does it matter? Learn your strengths. Understand your challenges. See yourself through other's eyes. How you see yourself may be quite different than the way other people see you. Find out where those perceptions are different and where they are similar. Why? Because you then have choices as to how you want others to see you and if you want to be seen as YOU and or someone living a life she was told she should live—instead of the one that is truly hers.

CHAPTER 1

NEVER WEAR RED

"WHAT WE THINK, WE BECOME."

BUDDHA

WE CAN BE OUR OWN worst enemy. We get in our own way. We listen to the naysayers... and begin to believe them. We unknowingly record experiences that cause us fear, uncertainty, anger, frustration, betrayal, rejection and so much more. We also record the good things about ourselves, but for many, the negatives outweigh the positives and have a most detrimental impact on our lives. If we let them.

This was never more true for me than when I was a kid. Kids can be the cruelest of all people. I remember walking through the halls of my school in the 7th grade where the boys stood lining the walls along the lockers, coming out of and going into classes and as I passed by, calling out and chanting, "I'd rather be dead than red in the head"; "hey carrot-top – what kind of a freak are you?"; and "look, it's Ronald McDonald in a skirt!" and added on to that were the "NEVER, NEVER WEAR RED!" from the OWKS; and, even from the teachers, "it's a good thing you're smart and athletic – at least you have that going for you" and it went on and on and on.

As most of us experience in one way or another as we are

Chapter 1 - Never Wear Red

growing up, there seems to be a litany of phrases and facts of things we should and should not say, do, dream about or pursue. Now don't misunderstand, for me and maybe for you, too, there were also a lot of encouraging words and phrases as well—but somehow, as a kid, all I ever really heard were the more powerful and negative messages. And after a while I started to believe them. I was not like other people; I could not be as smart, as successful, as cool, as anything. And to some extent, I became what I thought—and needed to fix it—always looking for something or someone outside of myself to make me right.

And then, about 30 years later, after surviving a series of personal and professional traumas and crises', I took a very deep and soul searching look inside—who was I really? And I started finding the answers. And you know what? I began to realize that those things were not true and I was a special person and it was about time I got over myself and believed it. I was too old to be buying into all of that from the past.

I was weary of listening to all the voices telling me to never wear red. That translated into don't try, you might fail. Don't risk, you might get hurt. Don't do that, you are not smart enough, don't dream that—you are foolish—you are being a Pollyanna. To this day, I am sensitive to that phrase—it somehow says you are not smart—you are not serious—you cannot be taken seriously—you are the red-headed step child—another favorite (not) phrase.

I looked in the mirror and said, "it's about time you started wearing red." Then I bought the most fabulous pair of red high heeled shoes that I could find. And that was the beginning of my journey of discovery—it was my coming out party. Finding my inner champion, my authentic self, my genuine leader.

Simply put, we cannot lead anyone or anything effectively until we first figure out who we are and why, then have the courage to be that person, 100% of the time.

Red shoes are my personal icon of inner power. They shout from the rooftops (at least in my head) that I am unique and that I have very special gifts.

I share all of this to help you find a better understanding and awareness of your genuine self. Examine your true strengths and challenges and form a clear vision of who, what, why, where and how you will guide and direct your own lives in your own way and in your own time. You need a Vision—you need to step up and take 100% responsibility and accountability for you and your life—and you need to know how to manifest a vision of who you want to become and what your life will be like and then support it with icons that are deeply meaningful to you in the here and now.

MANIFESTING VISION

Most people spend more time planning a two-week vacation than they do planning their lives or careers. And then they wonder why life never seems to turn out the way they want it to. Hmmm. Sound familiar? If it does, then perhaps it's time to start thinking about what you want your life to look like, who you want to become, and how to go about creating all of it!

And it all starts with a vision.

You Will Never Be Greater Than the Vision That Guides You.

> "THE VERY ESSENCE OF LEADERSHIP IS YOU HAVE TO HAVE A VISION. IT'S GOT TO BE A VISION THAT YOU ARTICULATE

CLEARLY AND FORCEFULLY ON EVERY OCCASION. YOU CAN'T BLOW AN UNCERTAIN TRUMPET."

FATHER THEODORE HESBURGH
FORMER PRESIDENT OF NOTRE DAME UNIVERSITY

Many years ago, I found myself in a job going nowhere and in a rather challenging place in my life and career. So, I wrote a vision statement of what I wanted my life to look like in 10-15 years. I was really specific and saw everything I wrote down, including the better version of myself that I would become. And then I found pictures and images that spoke to my vision and collected them into a collage that I looked at every day (and still do). The vision included things like: building a successful business; being in a wonderful relationship; having a dog; enjoying a rich social life; and the vision went on. I wrote it all in the present tense as if it had already happened. Guess what? All those things came true and life continues to get better as each year goes by.

THE POWER OF VISION

So, what does success look like to you? What is your vision?

Your vision is your quest—it is your written painting of what the future will look like—what you aspire to become, create and achieve. Begin everything with this end in mind, as this is the image by which everything else you do is measured.

WORDS

Write Your Vision Statement

This is a statement of what your life will look like in the future. Answer these questions to help you get started...

- Who are you?
- What is your purpose in life?
- What/who do you want to become?
- What do you want your life to be like?
- How do you see your relationships with
  - Yourself
  - Your Family
  - Your Friends
  - Your Business Associates
  - Your Community
  - The World
  - All Others

Write your vision in great detail, in the first person, in the present tense—as if it is already real.

- Find visuals to support it and make a collage.
- Create your goals around each facet of your vision.
- Then create the action steps necessary to fulfill those goals.
- Put the goals in a timeline for the short and long term.
- Keep a list of your goals accomplished.
- Look at it every day.
- Celebrate small victories!
- Stop trying to be what everyone else has told you to be and just be you.

 **GO FOR GOLD**

- Nothing is real until it is written. Write it down!
- Stop blaming yourself and others—step up and take accountability for your attitudes and behavior.
- Forgive.
- Take some time to really understand who you are and not what everyone else has been telling you to be. Pause—reflect. Take a walk.
- Find a personal icon of your power and purpose—red shoes work for me!

Take Action.

- Manifest your vision of what you want your life to be—and who you want to become—then write it down. Write it down in detail.

CHAPTER 2

0.2mg Gold

"In order to succeed, we must first believe that we can."

Nikos Kazantzakis

Every human being has 0.2mg of gold in their body. Most of this gold is in the heart. But it takes courage, will, desire and strength to mine this gold and unleash it for you to become the leader—the champion—you are meant to be.

This nugget of gold represents our special and unique purpose, our reason for being here. It can take a life-time for some to figure it out, if they ever do. And yet, for many, they have known it from the time they had conscious thought. And then for the rest, it happens somewhere along the road of our lives. I've always believed that we are given this life so that we can try to figure it all out (or least a good part of it) in a finite time frame. With each new awareness of ourselves and others, we evolve a bit more to a higher level of our own unique and authentic self.

And that's when we begin to discover the gold. That little nugget of magic that each one of us possesses and is unlike anyone else's. It is what we do (or can do) better than anyone else on the planet. I know. Hard to imagine such a thing, isn't? But it is true—the difficulty for us mere mortals is to figure out what it is and then, what the hell do we do with it?

Past, Present & Future

So, let's begin by taking the first steps to start mining our gold. We need to first look at our past (we are all products of our past in some way or another), then our present (where are you right now in this moment—how did you get here—and are you happy where you are or not?), and then the future—where do you see yourself in a week, a year, a lifetime?

Once we examine our past, present and future, then we need to ask ourselves some incredibly important questions. "Who is responsible for me? How did I get here? What do I like about myself and my life? What don't I like about myself and my life and who can I blame or praise?" Getting the idea? Right. There is only one person you can turn to—one person and one person only. You. Your successes and failures are not caused by external influences, people or events. 100% of both your accomplishments and failures are internally driven—by you, your thoughts and your attitude. Once you realize that and take responsibility for 100% of your life and decisions... the world starts to change.

And it changes in some rather significant, sometimes wild and crazy ways, if you allow your mind to be open. Taking 100% responsibility for yourself: being accountable to YOU all of the time takes first, awareness, then courage, then a plan and action to take you through each moment, day, week, year. Only when we take full accountability for ourselves, do we begin the journey of becoming a leader and the most genuine person we are meant to be.

I just cannot stress enough how important it is to gain real awareness and understanding of self. If we do not know who we really, truly are then we have no foundation for leading ourselves, let alone leading others!

There is a myriad of assessments on the market today that can help with this to at least get you started down the path of discovering and becoming the leader you are meant to be. I will make some recommendations for these later in this chapter.

Having a clear understanding of our values and principles, purpose, passion, dreams and vision will create a new way of thinking and behaving. Once we get truly on purpose and intentional about who we are and what are we doing with our lives, it's amazing what happens—we get a whole lot happier, more successful, confident and appreciative.

Let's begin. Open your mind.

More.

More.

More!

OK.

Where have you been?

- What are the milestones in your life thus far that have guided you to where you are today?
- Successes?
- Challenges?
- What have you learned and what decisions have you made as a result?
- Are you happy with your choices?
- Would you have done anything differently?
- What?
- Why?
- Have you—are you—moving toward what you want or away from what you don't?

- Why?
- Where are you now?
- Are you where you thought you would be at this point in time?
- Why?
- Why not?
- What motivates you?
- What inspires you?
- What do you want more of in your life?
- What do you want less of in your life?
- What is holding you back?
- Why?
- What are you attracting into your life?
- Where are you going?
- What is your vision of the future? Tomorrow? Next week? Next Year? 10 Years?
- What dreams have you forgotten about that you need to revisit?
- What do you want people to say about you in the future?
- How is that—or is it—different than what they say about you now?
- What will your legacy be?
- For your family?
- Friends?
- Colleagues?
- Business?

- Community?
- World?
- What is the most important thing you can do today to start shaping the future you envision?
- What's stopping you from doing it?
- Why?

We could go on and on with questions to trigger your thinking, but you get the idea. We need to very purposeful about what our lives are about—and how we impact others and the world around us. We have choices every day that impact our happiness and success; are you making the choices that drive your vision of the future?

If you have never done this kind of reflection before, it may be somewhat surprising to you to see the patterns in thinking and behavior that continue to come to the surface year after year. What do you think about these things? Are they good and moving you closer to your vision? Or are they confusing and taking you further away from your vision? Spend some time thinking about those patterns of thought and action that you like about your past, present and future; and those patterns of thought and action that you do not like about your past, present and future. Then, take a blank piece of paper, draw a vertical line down the middle. On the left, list the patterns and behaviors that have continually shown up in your life that you feel are good, positive, and taking you closer to your vision. On the right, list the patterns and behaviors that have continually shown up in your life that you feel are negative and taking you further away from your vision.

Now, ask yourself why? What are the positive thoughts, behaviors and actions that you feel good about and have a positive impact on your life and others? Is it patience? Listening skills? Clear communication? Where did you learn these positive behaviors? How can you consciously and intentionally bring more of these positive thoughts into your life on a daily basis?

And the same with the negative and limiting thoughts, behaviors and actions. What are they? You are not good enough, smart enough, good-looking enough, thin enough... that you are not enough? What are those self-inflicted limitations that you may not even be aware of and where do they come from and why?

For now, just give these questions some thought and jot down any comments, emotions or experiences they provoke. We'll revisit these questions throughout the book and begin to uncover some of the answers and insights that will begin to transform your idea of self and uncover your unique GOLD.

You First

Most of us have heard the analogy of the flight attendant's instructions before a flight—it goes something like this: "in the event of loss of cabin pressure, an oxygen mask will come down from the overhead area. Place the mask over your face first, and then help others." Put you first. That's the only way you will be able to help others. You have to have your own breath—your own focus—and know who you are before you can help others do the same.

Learn YOU first. When we take the time to really see ourselves from the inside out—it can be a real awakening. So, I suggest taking a pause and doing some assessments and self-reflection. In order to become the best version of ourselves, we need to start with an understanding of self!

A great way to start is with self-assessments, as well as 360's. These are enormously helpful and eye-opening. Some of the best ones that I use on a consistent basis include:

- Strengths Finder 2.0 by Tom Rath (http://www.strengthsfinder.com/home.aspx)
- The Hartman Color Code (https://www.**colorcode**.com/)
- DISC and VALUES Assessments. There are many different versions of the DISC assessment and VALUES-based assessments. It's a matter of which one you feel most comfortable with and if you will be working with a certified facilitator and/or coach. It is always my recommendation that you work with certified professionals on any kind of assessment to be sure you get the most out of the process.
- The LPI 360 – I use many different assessments, but I can say without hesitation that the Leadership Practices Inventory® (LPI) by Jim Kouzes and Barry Posner (A Wiley Company) is by far the best 360-degree instrument I have ever used. Based on over 30 years of research and quantifiable results, this is a tool that can transform individual leadership as well as entire cultures of leaderships. More information can be found at www.prolaureate.com; www.lpionline.com and www.theleadershipchallenge.com.

VALUES AND PRINCIPLES

Another critical piece in really understanding ourselves at the deepest levels is to think about what our values are and if and how we are living our lives in alignment with those values.

Chapter 2 - 0.2mg Gold

Have you ever thought about what is really guiding your decisions and actions at the deepest part of your soul? Why do you do the things you do? Do your decisions and actions make you feel good about yourself or not so good?

There are many versions of Values Assessment—The Leadership Challenge workshop uses Value Cards and here is one that we used in the women's leadership program, SOAR (Peer Exchange Network).

Take a moment to do the following—read through the list of words you see. Then, go back over the list and select the five words that jump out at you and resonate with you as your five core values.

Stop here and do not read any further until you have listed your five words either at the bottom of the next page or on a separate piece of paper. Once you do that, then you can read on.

Adaptability	*Discontent*
Justice	*Resilience*
Achievement	*Discretionary Time*
Knowledge	*Respect*
Accountability	*Diversity*
Leadership	*Results*
Advancement	*Empathy*
Learning	*Reverence*
Adventure	*Energy*
Listening	*Risk*
Attentiveness	*Enthusiasm*

Location	*Safely*
Authority	*Entrepreneurship*
Love	*Security*
Life Balance	*Environmental Awareness*
Loyalty	*Service*
Being the Best	*Ethics*
Make a Difference	*Status*
Belonging	*Fairness*
Meetings	*Social*
Breathing Space	*Faith*
Money	*Success*
Caring	*Family/Friends*
Opportunities	*Spiritual*
Challenge	*Focus*
Organization	*Team*
Collegiality	*Forgiveness*
Growth	*Territory*
Comfort	*Friendship*
Partnering	*Tolerance*
Commitment	*Harmony*
Peace	*Tradition*
Communication	*Honesty*
Positive Spirit	*Trust*
Community	*Humor/Fun*
Power	*Unity*
Compassion	*Improvement*

Prestige	*Vacations*
Competition	*Independence*
Profit	*Variety*
Confidence	*Influence*
Productivity	*Vision*
Contribution	*Information*
Purpose	*Wealth*
Control	*Initiative*
Quality	*Wisdom*
Cooperation	*Innovation*
Recognition	*Creativity*
Integrity	*Relationships*
Customer Focus	*Intelligence*
Relaxation	*Dignity*
Involvement	*Reliability*

MY INDIVIDUAL VALUE SET

_____

_____

Now, look at the five values you chose, and remove two of them—leaving the three values you would fight for. Go ahead—do not read any further until you have narrowed your values to the three you would **fight** for.

Good. Now, go back again and remove two more, leaving the ONE value you would **die** for and write it here in large letters:

This is your core value. The thing that is the most important to you and that all else falls under. Without this one thing, your life would be meaningless.

Now, ask yourself if you have made—and continue to make—all of your decisions in alignment to your core value. Do your decisions take you closer to your core value or further away? Do your actions mirror your core value or do they contradict it?

My core value is a four-letter word. It's a really scary word to a lot of people. Some of them even get irritated, agitated, embarrassed, offended or totally put-off by the word and me when I talk about it. That's OK.

The word is **LOVE**. It guides my entire life and all of my decisions and actions. Whenever I am in doubt about what do to or how to do it—I always go back to love. Is my action/decision in the best interest of the people around me? Will this let them know I care about them and their well - being? Is this being driven by pure love for my fellow human beings and doing what is right for them regardless of the potential harm or risk or pain or whatever that it may bring to me?

Now please don't misunderstand this is no way about being a martyr, or a Mother Theresa, or a Dali Lama, I am in no way that good, smart or selfless. It is, however, about holding myself and others to the fire of accountability—of not being a victim—of not blaming everything and everyone but ourselves for where we are right now, right here in this very moment. That's the love

I am talking about, the tough love it takes to be honest and to be truly the best of ourselves. This, along with a good dose of compassion and empathy is what creates understanding, growth and development of our best selves. It's the beginning of your leadership love story.

Amazing.

PURPOSE & PASSION

Which brings us to our driving purpose and passion. This self-discovery stuff is rather astonishing once you get the hang of it. When you start to really examine your values, decisions and actions—and how aligned you really are to what is most important to you—a funny thing happens. You find your true purpose and passion.

Many years ago, I worked in a small but extremely successful business. I was part of an amazing group of people. We worked hard. We played hard. But most of all, we loved what we did and the people we worked with, our colleagues; and the people we worked for—our customers and clients. We were dedicated to bringing the highest quality of products and services to all those with whom we worked, but more than that, we were committed to always going the extra mile. Always.

We respected each other. We trusted each other. We were all about helping our people, customers, vendors, families, communities and colleagues grow and build their success. We understood and appreciated that the relationships we built were why we were in the business in the first place.

As I look back on those 12 years at the company, I can tell you that it was the single most important time in my career and life at that point. In many ways, I grew up there. Traveled the world. I learned what I did best in the world. Made lifelong friends. Became part of an amazing Executive Team. Helped to put a small company on the map—the global map.

That was about 10 years in. Then we were bought out by a $60 billion behemoth global company because they could not compete with us. We were the little engine that DID, and they wanted us.

Nevertheless, during the initial acquisition negotiations, I kept asking if anyone was conducting a leadership and cultural due diligence on the merger of the two organization's values, vision, mission, people, culture, customers, demographics, etc. I was ignored—no wait, not ignored—I was shushed.

Of course, that didn't work, I spoke up anyway. To the point that I was sure they would fire me once the acquisition was complete and the merger was underway. And I did not care. What I was seeing was abhorrent.

They were destroying not just a business, but a family of some of the most dedicated people on the planet—and along with it, the culture and success that I had been a part of creating and the people with it. It was bad. It was ugly. It was unnecessary. And yet it happened. They were telling me to help them do it. This was just business.

Well it was not the kind of business I was ever in nor wanted to be in—ever. So I left. Took some time to sort through what had happened and where I wanted to go from there. And what I realized was that we had created a culture of genuine, authentic leadership from the ground up. And it drove the growth and success of the business and the respect of our colleagues and customers world-wide.

Chapter 2 - 0.2mg Gold

We had become champions—not in an egotistical way—but in a musketeer way, all for one and one for all. We had found our own leadership best in ourselves and in each other and lived it every day.

So with this in mind, I began to write and think and write some more and asked myself this question: "what was the one thing I had been doing in every job and every relationship I ever had throughout my entire life that was effortless, natural and had a profound impact on others and my own development?"

It took me a long time to answer that question, and I made a lot of mistakes along the way, but I finally figured it out. As corny as it sounds, I have always helped other people to become the best of who they are meant to be—if that is what they want. I never realized that this was a gift, I just figured everyone thought that way. But when I did begin to realize that this is, and always has been, my core belief, value, motivation, purpose, passion and God-given gift, then I needed to figure out how to do it on purpose—with intention—and for the rest of my life.

This experience crystallized my purpose, passion, values and why. If you would like to know more about these and how they formed the foundation of my company and my life, go to www.prolaureate.com and take a look under the WHY tab—it's our GOLD.

And so, ProLaureate emerged. The word ProLaureate is one I created. It means "Professional Laureate." We all know the terms Baccalaureate; Poet Laureate; Nobel Laureate; and so on. The term Laureate comes from the ancient Greeks. They would crown those who achieved exemplary success and knowledge in a field of study or in competitive events (the beginning of the Olympic Games) with a crown of laurel leaves. And once crowned, they were then a Laureate.

From Wikipedia:

> Bay laurel was used to fashion the laurel wreath of ancient Greece, a symbol of highest status. A wreath of bay laurels was given as the prize at the Pythian Games because the games were in honor of Apollo, and the laurel was one of his symbols.
>
> The symbolism carried over to Roman culture, which held the laurel as a symbol of victory.[14] It is also the source of the words baccalaureate and poet laureate, as well as the expressions "assume the laurel" and "resting on one's laurels".

So I began to dream about Professional Champions.... **ProLaureates.**

DREAMS

When was the last time you actually just dreamed—without limitations? Probably since you were a kid. As we get older and take on more and more filters in the way we think; we allow our experiences to overshadow possibility; and we forget how to dream. Dream with abandon and dream with no limitations. Think—what would you do if you knew you would not fail? What would you do if there were no limitations (real or imagined) on who or what or where or how you could do, be, or become anything you wanted?

Start creating a Dream Inventory. Your first list should include at least 25 dreams. They can be dreams about anything! Those you had as a child; wishes you know will never happen or come true, hopes that are as outlandish as you care to make them, dreams you know are just out of your reach, but attainable—anything goes here! Stretch your mind and imagination. These can be dreams about what you want to have, do or become, where you want to go, what you want to drive, where you want to live, how you want to be known, how you want to be remembered. The sky is the limit! The purpose of this is to start exercising one of the biggest and most neglected parts of your being—your brain! We have so much capacity to create the lives we want, we just forget how as we grow into adults. Now is the time to start again!

Once you have your Dream Inventory started, keep adding to it every day and every week. Challenge yourself to see how many you can come up with. Then go to this YouTube video by Malcom Cohan and create your own video vision statement:

https://www.youtube.com/watch?v=miIs1clQ5EM

This really does work. It will play a very important part as you emerge and begin to put a plan in place to become that very best version of yourself.

Focus

Now that you are beginning to find your passion—that one thing that you do better than anyone else in the world, it's time to focus. Time to focus on why, how and what you are about—thank you to Simon Sinek for his concept of the Golden Circles. Go to Simon's site www.simonsinek.com and watch his TedTalk "Start With Why".

And then, write yours.

Start with your WHY.

Here's mine:

I believe there is a heart of gold—a hero, a champion, a leader— inside each and every one of us.

I believe this champion has the power to transform our lives; help us become the best version of ourselves and create a life of happiness and success beyond our wildest dreams.

And I also believe that we can be our own worst enemy when it comes to actually letting that Champion emerge. We get in our own way.

My 'why' is to work with others to help them find their inspiration, ignite it with passion and planning... and then impact their lives, the lives of others and the world in amazing ways all by unleashing their gold and emerging as a champion.

This is genuine, authentic leadership.

I have re-invented myself at least 5 times in my lifetime so far and am in the process of doing so again as I write this! From the little red-haired girl; to the tomboy playing baseball and hockey with her big brother and the boys; to the big sister of a little sister who is 11 years younger; to the high school honors student who had moved 22 times by the time she graduated; to the college kid working her way through school with no clue of what she would become; to the actress; to the corporate executive; to the entrepreneur; to the wife of an entrepreneur and step-mom of five kids; to the coach, author and speaker—all of these iterations have taken me ever closer to, well, me. And what a great place to be!

So, what about you? Are you ready to step up and go for gold?

 **GO FOR GOLD**

- We are all products of our past, but we don't have to stay there. Learn from the past, live in the present and design your own future—be the captain of your own ship. What have you learned so far? How are you using that knowledge to make better decisions? To be accountable?
- Discover what really inspires you and do more of it more often. Make a living from it if you can, but by all means take the time to figure out what it is and then spend time in that space. You have qualities and talents that no one else on the planet does or ever will. Use them.
- Know thyself. Become self-aware. Take assessments, they are fun and you can learn all kinds of cool thinks about yourself and about others.

Actions:
- Hire a coach.
- Get a mentor.
- Take a 360—find out what your co-workers and colleagues really think about your leadership style.
- Write down your non-negotiable values and principles and live by them every day. Walk your talk.
- Dream. Dream some more. Keep dreaming. Wake up that inner-child and let him or her get out and play. Have fun and let your imagination run wild. You might be amazed at what you think of and what shows up in your life.

- Get crystal clear on your focus. Write it down.
- Reinvention is good. Make a plan. Follow it. Do it. Often.

CHAPTER 3

GRIT

"FAILURE IS UNIMPORTANT. IT TAKES COURAGE TO MAKE A FOOL OF YOURSELF."

CHARLIE CHAPLAN

I wish I had a dime for every time I was faced with an obstacle, a bully, a problem, a defeat, a heartbreak, a disappointment, a ne'er-do-well. I'd be very wealthy. I'll bet it is the same for you. But if wishes were horses, beggars would ride. So instead—use all the sticks and stones that have been hurled at you throughout your life at this point—to strengthen your resolve and your inner courage and determination to be and to become the very best YOU, you can be. These are invaluable lessons my friends. It may not seem like it in the moment, but when you can look at them that way, then ask yourself every time: "what do I need to learn from this," "how can I use this to move closer to my vision and even more clearly define who I am in my most genuine, unique and special way?" You always have a choice and you are always 100% responsible for where you have been, where you are and where you are going—no one else—just you. Here's just one of those stories:

THE BOARD ROOM

Remember that story I shared earlier about the company I was with for 12 years? Well here is how it all finally came to a close for me.

There were 12 men and me in a Board Room. They were deciding next steps for the company—the strategy, the territories, the markets, the production and products, et al—and they were starting down a very slippery slope.

The discussion was not really about any of those things listed above, nor was it about wise and smart strategy based on solid values, principles and foresight. Those were just the red herrings. It was really all about ego. It was about who was smartest, held the title, had the power, could overrule everyone else. It was not about moving a solid, profitable and successful company to new levels of success—for the people and the company.

The arguments continued, I continued to try and intervene to express my views and ideas, and I continued to be shushed; pushed off to the side and ignored. Not one of those men would even look me in the eye, let alone recognize my voice and comments. It was at that point, that I realized I would never be heard. I also realized that the new owners did not share the same values or vision that we did—it was crystal clear to me that I was in a place that was a total contradiction to who I was and what I believed. After all these years, I knew I could not stay. It would tear me apart inside and I would be yet another worker bee doing work and doing it in a way that ran contrary to every value and belief that I held dear.

These are defining moments. This is when you know you must take a stand—when courage rises to the surface regardless of the repercussions and you make decisions that can be, and many times should be, life changing.

And so I did. At the risk of being dramatic, my soul was in jeopardy. I could no longer be a part of what was happening. My decision was made. I stood up. Look around the room in silence. Eventually the conversation stopped and they looked at me as if to say, "What are you doing? Sit down." At least I had gotten their attention. Then I looked each of them in the eye, and said: "Gentlemen, I suggest we take a break. Let's all leave the room and when we come back, park all egos outside the door. Then we can have a meaningful conversation about the future of the company based on the business at hand."

Amazingly, they did. Nonetheless, I had drawn my line in the sand and was fully aware of the consequences. I was darn sure I would be fired, I probably would have fired me, so I went to my office and starting packing my things. My CEO followed me. He did not fire me, but thanked me and asked me to stay on for a while. He said someone had to say something in the meeting to get it on the right track and I was the only who did.

As I look back on that, it was a turning point for me - one that completely changed the trajectory of my life and career. And it was all based on my 0.2 mg of gold—my grit. I knew the situation was no longer where I belonged. I had to make a change. I was scared to death. I did it anyway.

In retrospect, and with all I have learned, studied and practiced over the years, and continue to do so, I would have handled the situation somewhat differently, perhaps with a bit more emotional intelligence, but the outcome would have been the same.

I stayed on for a while to help make the transition to the new company and look out for my team, but then I moved on.

Defining moments.

That day and that moment was a turning point for me. I knew who I was and who I was not and was willing to put it all on the line. There are moments in life when you just know—know that you are facing a turning point and you either step up or you don't—and you will live with whatever decision you make, forever. Grit.

The lessons I learned were invaluable. And I apply them every day. They helped form the foundation of my company and strengthened me in the process. This experience was one of many that led me to my true self, my courage and my grit. And I will forever be grateful. And will forever continue to work on becoming a better me.

COURAGE

It takes courage to live your own life in your own way – to look the naysayers and the bullies in the eye and not stand down. It takes courage to take 100% accountability for yourself. It takes courage to be a champion and your best self.

> "WHAT MAKES A KING OUT OF A SLAVE? COURAGE! WHAT MAKES THE FLAG ON THE MAST TO WAVE? COURAGE! WHAT MAKES THE ELEPHANT CHARGE HIS TUSK IN THE MISTY MIST, OR THE DUSKY DUSK? WHAT MAKES THE MUSKRAT GUARD HIS MUSK? COURAGE! WHAT MAKES THE SPHINX THE SEVENTH WONDER? COURAGE! WHAT MAKES THE DAWN COME UP LIKE THUNDER? COURAGE! WHAT

Chapter 3 - Grit

> MAKES THE HOTTENTOT SO HOT? WHAT PUTS THE 'APE' IN APRICOT? WHAT HAVE THEY GOT THAT I AIN'T GOT?
>
> COURAGE!"
>
> **THE COWARDLY LION**
> **THE WIZARD OF OZ**

They say that fear is the greatest inhibitor of success. Sometimes it's fear of failure and sometimes it's fear of success. But whichever it is, we need to understand it deep within ourselves in order to overcome it. Remember courage is not the absence of fear. It is being afraid and stepping up anyway! It is doing what you know is right, not easy or acceptable to others, but what you know is right for you—in your heart, mind and soul.

Sir Winston Churchill proclaimed that, "Courage is the first of human qualities because it is the quality that guarantees all others."

This is not about being a hero. It's about facing challenges both big and small: speaking up when it would be easier to remain silent, to work when you don't particularly feel up to it, and to attack your problems until they are solved.

Courage is like leadership. We learn it. We need to understand what it is and how to use it and practice it every day. That's the only way we get good at anything, right? Practice! And once you get the hang of it—it's totally empowering—in a quiet, strong kind of way. It builds confidence, not ego, and allows us to clear the fog of conflict and confusion of the red herrings that get throw in our path. And it all starts with knowing truly and genuinely who we really are and what we stand for.

Just ask the Lion...

"Read what my medal says:

"Courage".

Ain't it the truth?

Ain't it the truth?"

Again, courage is not the absence of fear—it is facing the fear and doing what you need and want to do anyway. Courage is overcoming fear and moving through it. That is the key to courage!

There is an old saying that I heard a lot as a kid. Whenever I hit a rough patch—whether it was failing a test, being made fun of by the other kids, not making the cheerleading squad, or just feeling sorry for myself, my Mom would always say "Roxanne Marie, pull yourself up by your bootstraps and get busy!"

Now we know that in the physical world, we really cannot reach down and lift ourselves off the ground by pulling on our bootstraps, but the metaphor makes sense. Its simple wisdom. It's simply profound. We are responsible for every moment in our lives. We are accountable for where we are in this very moment—no one else.

We need to get over ourselves, take responsibility for our lives and just get on with it. It's a simple principle of leadership—we will fail, we will fall, we will miss the mark—it's a human being thing. And if we don't, we are not growing and learning. Leadership is in the lesson. Pulling ourselves up and out is the behavior. Growing into more of who we truly are is the result.

As Jim Kouzes and Barry Posner, founders of The Leadership Challenge® tell us: "the greatest leaders are the greatest learners."

Chapter 3 - Grit

What did we learn and what will we do with it? The lessons that are the toughest, that hurt the most, that drive us to the brink are the ones that test our mettle, our strength, our determination, our gold.

That's when a leader pulls up their boot straps and digs in with grit.

http://www.huffingtonpost.com/news/women-in-the-boardroom/

Trust

I have never met anyone who did not have a story to tell about trust. Whether it be about the bond and strength that real trust brings to a relationship, a family, a business or how the lack of trust or destruction of trust can be so devastating on so many levels.

Many years ago, I worked with a fellow that I considered to be among my best friends and confidantes. We had worked together for several years and were both on the Executive Team. We were in a meeting one day with the people that were buying our company when the conversation turned to what I knew would be a disastrous direction for the business.

I voiced my thoughts clearly with an explanation as to why I felt this way and was quickly shushed—again—while the others continued the conversation. I was embarrassed, of course, but more importantly, I was concerned, shocked and upset the conversation was allowed to continue down such a destructive and potentially unethical path. Later that evening, my friend and I had dinner together and I expressed my frustration and concern from the meeting, and knowing that I was in 'safe' company, allowed myself to cry.

The next day, the meeting reconvened and the conversation from the previous day came up again. Before anyone could say a word, my friend laughed out loud and said, "better not bring that up again, boys, Roxanne might end up in the corner crying."

Broken trust. Betrayal. Humiliation. In that moment, a relationship of many years ended. As we have all heard before—it takes years to build trust and a second to destroy it. And once it is broken it's like trying to unwrinkle a wadded-up piece of paper. It cannot be done. The creases will always remain.

I did confront this person one-on-one after the meeting. I followed him into the hall and asked him to step outside with me. In a very quiet and steady voice, eyeball to eyeball, I said, "I am not angry for what you just did in there. But I am furious that you just destroyed our friendship and that I can never trust you again. You have broken my trust and our friendship. I never knew you were so small that you had to bring someone else down so you could feel big." The end.

We all have our trust stories—the good, the bad and the ugly and although they can be so terribly painful, what's important is what we learn and take away from them. I did not walk away from that thinking I would never trust someone again, but I did walk away learning to trust myself more. To stand up for who and what I am. To expect respect because I earn it and to not let others pull me into their own mire of ego games. To face betrayal head-on and then move on.

Do not allow yourself to be bullied in any way, shape or form. It steals your self-worth if you let it.

Chapter 3 - Grit

WORTHINESS

I have been on the Board and serve as a volunteer for an organization called Margeau's Free To Be Project since 2012. This organization came about when a dear friend's daughter of 29 years of age died from feelings of unworthiness. This lack of self-worth manifested itself in many debilitating ways for this beautiful young woman until her body just could not take it anymore.

Tragic. How many of us have allowed this lack of worthiness to rob us of our inner life? I did for a long time. Thankfully, I survived it and much more than that—I have thrived because of it in many ways. But that is sadly not always the case.

What stories do you have; what experiences have you had that have robbed you of your self-worth? People making less of you so they can feel more and so many other ways people are unkind and sometimes devastatingly cruel. Remember when this does happen—it is not about you. It is about them.

Even then, we remember these egregious events. Unfortunately, these events impact us in many ways and stay with us. They seep into our souls to some extent and it hurts us—takes a chunk out of our self-esteem and worthiness whether we realize it or not.

As my friend Gail would say about her daughter Margeau, she believed in everyone but herself. We are all born worthy—it's our birthright. WE HAVE THE GOLD WITHIN US! We just need to recognize it and embrace it. Do not let others take away your own self-worth. Do not be a victim. Know that you are perfect just the way you are and everything you need to be the rock star you were born to be is already inside you!

Another organization that I have been involved with since its inception is a national leadership conference called 'Woman of Power'. It's founder, Raquel Eatmon, is indeed the quintessential woman of power. She is a friend of the highest order, a soul sister and respected colleague. She started this movement with a passion and purpose to lift women into an awareness of their own worthiness and personal power and then help them learn how to apply that awareness to their lives and careers. Raquel has created a 'leadership movement' of incredible scope and impact. More information can be found at raqueleatmon.com and ProjectHeard.com.

There are so many resources available to us from thought leaders on all aspects of leadership. Take some time to investigate and find the ones that speak to you and can guide you to find and develop your own potential.

Here is a link to a good article by Deepak Chopra on betrayal and the whole trust and worthiness issue.

http://www.oprah.com/spirit/What-to-Do-When-Youve-Been-Betrayed-Deepak-Chopra

At this point, you have paused. Started to think about and become more aware of your strengths, talents, passions and maybe even your purpose. At the very least, you are beginning to understand a bit more about how your brain works and how you are wired and are you are thinking about the answers and lessons you can take away from various experiences in your life. Great!

What does all this have to do with wearing red and getting ahead? Everything.

THE GLASS CEILING

"The term 'glass ceiling' was coined in a 1986 Wall Street Journal report on corporate women by Hymowitz and Schellhardt. The glass ceiling is a concept that most frequently refers to barriers faced by women who attempt, or aspire, to attain senior positions (as well as higher salary levels) in corporations, government, education and nonprofit organizations. It can also refer to racial and ethnic minorities and men when they experience barriers to advancement." **The Glass Ceiling: Domestic and International Perspectives. Nancy Lockwood, SPHR, GPHR HR Content Expert.**

Does it exist or doesn't it? It depends. On who you are and what the circumstances are in your environment. And what do you do about it if it does? Raquel Eatmon, Founder and CEO of Rising Media, LLC and The Woman of Power™ National Leadership Conference, asked that question to an all-male panel at the 2015 Woman of Power event. The answers were surprising. One of the panelists, Robert Klonk, President and CEO of Oswald Companies, responded, "if there is a glass ceiling... break it." While I agree and rally to that sentiment, it is sometimes easier said than done.

But breaking it—actually shattering it is a much better approach in my opinion—is critical to your success. Pick your battles carefully and well, including the timing, and then be smart, savvy, determined and kind while you bring the damn thing down. Here are some suggestions and tools to shatter the ceiling:

- Find a mentor—man or woman, but someone you admire and will take the time to talk and meet with you on a regular basis to guide and share experiences with you.

- Be politically savvy—there is absolutely nothing wrong with being political, it is actually a huge talent but you must be genuine and authentic about it, not manipulative or scheming.
- Be self-aware—know how your behavior, words, actions and presence impact others. Do not assume you know the answers, ask them. Take a 360° assessment and/or other assessments to really understand your own behavior and increase your self-awareness.
- Communicate effectively. If you don't know how, take a class—learn
- Trust
- Give your power to others
- Build a clear, strong, unique personal brand that tells the world who you are, why you are, and what you are

Personal Brand

You are one-of-a-kind! Your personal brand should reflect that uniqueness. This is one of the most powerful tools for a leader—a strong, powerful and authentic personal brand. Why? It separates you from everyone else and allows others to see and appreciate your unique talents and the value you bring to the world. It also goes a long way in building your self-confidence and self-esteem.

A story:

A father and his two sons were out one Saturday afternoon doing some downtown shopping. When they finished, they decided to stop for lunch at the local diner. They walked down main street heading toward the diner, and stopped in the center

Chapter 3 - Grit

of town at the intersection to wait for the red light to change so they could cross the street.

As they waited and talked about what they were going to have for lunch, the shops they wanted to visit and what they wanted to buy, they became distracted by a sound coming from somewhere in the distance. As the sound got louder they stopped talking and looked and listened intently in the direction of the sound. It became louder and louder until, around the corner of the street came a guy on a motorcycle pulling up to the red light.

The sound of the motorcycle's engine was deep, rumbling and resonate. The sidewalk was vibrating under the boy's feet as the biker waited for the light to change.

They were mesmerized. The sight ... the sound... awesome. The light changed to green. The rider gave the bike a huge rev of the engine and then rumbled off into the distance.

The Dad had a knowing smile on his face as he and the boys watched the man ride away.

The young brothers were still staring after him long after the biker was out of view, when finally, little brother Sam, with a huge sigh, looked up and said to his big brother,

"Wow, Joey, did you see that motorcycle?"

Joey looked down at his little brother, paused, and simply said,

"That's not a motorcycle, Sam...

that's a Harley".

From the Harley Davidson website:

"*Harley Davidson motorcycles have evolved into so much more than just a brand name since their early 1900 beginnings. Their humble American start laid the ground work for the reputation of hardworking [people] and original [brand that] the Harley Davidson motorcycle still has today. Motorcyclists embrace this originality and express it in an outlaw, subculture society that appeals to a lot of humanity.*

Part of what makes the Harley Davidson motorcycle so alluring is its rich heritage and vibrant history. It began when a gentleman had a blue print for a engine that could fit in a bicycle frame. His friend decided to help him. The William S. Harley and Arthur Davidson – Harley Davidson Motor Company had been established."

Your personal brand is the culmination of every aspect of your life and experience—and most importantly, what you value. Your brand is what people think without thinking when they hear or see you or your name.

Your brand is not what you do, it is who you are. What you do is only a part of your brand—an important one, but only one part among many, many others.

Nike, Mercedes, Coke, Rolex, Tiffany's they all conger up an instant feeling, emotion, about what that brand means and only a small part of that feeling is about the product—the what. It is mostly about how the what makes us FEEL.

And your personal brand is no different. It leaves an imprint. It has an impact. It has a remembrance quotient. It all depends upon how you purposefully and intentionally build your brand.

Harley doesn't sell motorcycles they sell "rebel" (this is actually a written part of their branding strategy), and they have mastered multi-generational branding; much like Nike— you don't even need to see their name to get it, just the swoosh;

Mercedes doesn't sell cars (well, they kind of do now, but never used to) they sell top-of-the-line luxury and precision engineering; Coke is not a soft drink, it's the real thing; and Rolex doesn't sell watches they sell prestige and elegance and Tiffany's—well, you get the idea.

So what does your personal brand say about you? Your personal brand touches everything you do and everything you do touches the brand. It's a lot like attitude—it's your advance person—it shows up before you do. Every time someone comes into contact with your brand the brand is being enhanced and built, or eroded and taken apart, it depends upon those who come in contact with it have a positive or negative experience with your brand.

In a business sense, your personal brand is part of your business brand—it is you, your people, your beliefs, your values, your principles, your strategy, the way the phones are answered, the way problems are handled, the way correspondence is dealt with EVERYTHING is your brand. Whether in person, with an ad, a press release, a conversation with one of your people, through a product experience, a phone call or email with your offices, a visit to your website, reading an article in the paper or a journal, everything on social media, and a casual conversation with someone else who has experienced your brand, and their comments about it.

The Brand is the unique place you own in the mind of others. Be consistent. Own it. It represents everything you stand for, everything you do and everything you are—at every touch point—whether that be good or bad. When it's good, the more touch points the better.

We all have unique talents, characteristics, qualities and values that define who we are—these are the elements of your brand. The way we walk, talk, dress, shake hands, work, build relationships, and so on are all parts of our personal brand. What is yours? Are you a motorcycle or a Harley? Are you a presence or a shadow? What do you want your brand to say about you? Your brand and your attitude enter a room before you do, so be sure you know what it is and what it is not. It can make you or break you.

 **GO FOR GOLD**

Obstacles
- What is getting in your way of accomplishing what you want to accomplish?
- What can you do to overcome these barriers?
- Make a plan, write it down. What are you trying to achieve?
- What are the rewards of accomplishing your objectives?
- What are the consequences if you do not?
- What are the solutions and what action steps do you need to take?

Courage
- Courage is not the absence of fear. It is doing what needs to be done in spite of your fear. It is standing up for yourself, your values, your beliefs and accepting 100% of the consequences.

- What are you afraid of?
- Why?
- Be honest. Break your fears down and figure out what is behind them and take one at a time.

Trust

- It will be found—it will be given—and it will be broken. It is a gift and one to be treasured. Visit <u>www.becauseisaidiwould.com</u>.
- Give trust and accept it.
- Know when to hold 'em, know when to fold 'em, and know when to walk away.

Worthiness

- Believe in yourself. We are born worthy. KNOW that you are worthy of everything life has to offer. You just have to summon the will to make it happen. You are responsible for you.

Glass Ceiling

- Imagined or real—don't break it. Shatter it. And remember that sometimes the glass ceiling is one we have put there ourselves. Get out of your own way.

Brand

- Define your personal brand—you are one of a kind—you are totally unique with special talents and skills. Unleash your best self on the world, amazing things will happen.

- Write down, in detail, what your personal brand looks like, feels like, hears like, smells like and then create it. Wash, rinse, repeat. Make sure this brand reflects your most genuine and authentic self—that's what gives it the energy, the power, the impact.

CHAPTER 4

CROSS THE RIVER AND BURN THE BOAT

> "I CAN'T THINK OF ANYONE I ADMIRE WHO ISN'T FUELED BY SELF-DOUBT. IT'S AN ESSENTIAL INGREDIENT. IT'S THE GRIT IN THE OYSTER."
>
> **RICHARD EYRE**

IF FIVE FROGS ARE SITTING on a log and one decides to jump off, how many are left on the log?

Wait for it... Five.

The frog only decided to jump, he did not actually do it. Deciding to do something is not doing it. Just because I decided to put a treadmill in the basement doesn't mean I will get fit—I actually have to get on the thing and do something.

All of this takes motivation—internal motivation—and the desire to act. And it takes a decision to make something happen—with no excuses, entitlement or bail-outs—you must cross the river and burn the boat. No going back. Do it because you said you would.

When I left the corporation, and started down the path of that particular journey of reinvention, I had no idea where I was going, what I was going to do or how. I spent a lot of time reflecting on what I had learned so far, what I was not seeing, and figuring out what I was really passionate about and wanted to accomplish.

And that's when I realized that leadership had always been and continued to be my passion. I had seen what happens in life and businesses when leadership was its best and worst and I knew I wanted to help has many people and organizations learn the former and not have to experience the latter.

However, it takes more than just an aha moment or a realization of what you truly want to do and become to make it happen. You must DO something. You must JUMP! And, it takes an attitude of no turning back. You must be willing to give it your all—come what may! You need to cross the river and burn the boat. No going back, no retreat, no safe harbor, it is full steam ahead.

At least for me, that was the only way I knew I could succeed and it helped me focus and prioritize from the get-go. There is no silver bullet! It's hard work, but oh my it is worth it! To finally be in a place and in a space that you OWN, you created, and you love. A space where you are your most genuine self, doing what you do best—it just doesn't get any better than that.

What is the biggest obstacle to making this happen for yourself? As much as I don't want to tell you—the biggest obstacle is most likely YOU. Here's why.

MOTIVATION & CONDITIONING

There are two kinds of motivation—external and internal.

External motivation starts early in life and follows us for the rest of our lives, "eat your peas and you can have dessert." "Get all

A's and B's and you can have that toy." "Make your sales quota and you'll get the raise." "If you don't complete the project on time, you will not get the promotion." And so on. It's the old carrot and stick way of motivating people to do things or not do things.

External motivation is the "I have to."

Internal motivation is the "I want to."

When was the last time you were doing something that was so engaging, so much fun and so fulfilling that you totally lost track of time? You picked up your head and looked at the clock and hours had gone by? Whatever that activity was—you were engaged in it with great internal motivation.

This is the kind of motivation we need to pay attention to! What are those things that drive you in this way? These are things you love, that are in your sweet spot, that align to your talents, gifts, interests, passions and meaning. Do more of this and less of the other—wake up!

We are all so conditioned to so many things in our lives that become habit, we don't even know we are doing it, nor do we realize how self-limiting this is—we get in our own way. What are some of the things you do out of habit that you don't even realize you are doing?

How many of those things are sucking the energy and life out of your success, growth, progress, relationships and enjoyment?

Take a moment to track where you spend your time every day. What are you doing out of habit and conditioning and what are you doing intentionally and purposefully. What you find may surprise you!

Conditioning can create attitudes that we are unaware of, but that drive our thoughts. And those thoughts drives our behavior.

Conditioning comes from many different sources. One of the sources is in the way we grow up and the influences in our lives. Much of this in our early years is to protect us as we are growing up. But caution! Some of this can end up being very negative in terms of our own growth and success—and we don't even know It's happening.

Here are some examples of conditioning. Let's talk about frogs again. If you put a frog in a pot of boiling water—he will jump right out. But, if you put the frog in a pot of cold water and slowly heat the pot until it boils, the frog will not get out and will meet an unhappy demise. Why? Because the heat crept up on him so slowly he did not know he was in trouble.

What is slowly heating up in your life that you are not even aware of that may be putting obstacles and barriers in your way?

When they train baby elephants to stay within the paddock, they chain their leg to a tree or post, so the elephant can only go so far to the edge of the paddock area. The elephant grows up walking to the end of his tether and is stopped every time. He learns the limit of how far he can go. This continues into maturity for the elephant and then the chain is removed. How far do you think the elephant strays out of the paddock once the chain is removed? He doesn't. He doesn't know that he can go any further than what he has been conditioned to all of his life. He has been conditioned to stay within the range of the chain— and can go no further. What are the invisible chains holding you back from realizing your potential?

What is preventing you from doing what you dream of doing, becoming who you most genuinely are, going where you desire to go in both your personal and professional life. What are your chains? If you are not sure, ask those who are closest to you what they think you are doing to limit yourself. And be sure to thank them when they do. As hard as it is to hear, honest feedback is a gift.

We'll talk about this more in chapter 6 when I explain the Formula for Success, but for now, write down what you think your most limiting thoughts, attitudes and behaviors are that are preventing you from what you really want. Keep that list handy. You may want to add a few more as we go along.

Forgiveness

Becoming aware of our self-limiting thinking and behavior can be daunting. It often times requires a good dose of forgiveness to get our arms how we need to change to move forward.

Forgiveness is a big part of finding the strength, courage, awareness and power to cross whatever your 'river' may be and not look back. I know you are wondering why forgiveness comes into any this. It does and in an incredibly important and life-changing way. When I came to understand this and act upon it, it was a turning point for me.

Not unlike most humans, I've had my moments of regret, anger, disappointment and oh, so much more. I looked outside myself for the reasons and the solutions. Most of us, at one time or another and some more than others, blame the world, circumstances and other humans for what we did not achieve, did not do, did not decide, did not get, did not have and how we felt as a result.

What I have come to understand is that feeling that way and looking outside of ourselves for all the things that are wrong with our lives is a complete waste of time and energy. There is only one person who is responsible for you and your life. That person looks back at you every day in the mirror. Each of us is 100% responsible for ourselves. No one else. No one is entitled to anything. Each of us must earn our way through this world and this life. But first, before we can honestly step out and do any of this and take full accountability for ourselves—we must forgive ourselves.

Forgive yourself for your failures and your triumphs. Forgive yourself for not being who everyone has told you to be. Forgive yourself for bad choices, wrong decisions, course corrections, uncertainty, fear, feelings of loss and aloneness—and forgive yourself for understanding, listening, caring, being vulnerable, being smart, being whoever you truly are—forgive yourself.

And then, forgive others for all of the above.

This is what allows you to be in the world without judgement, criticism, negativity and loss. It sounds somewhat mystical or perhaps spiritual and maybe it is, but to me it's just common sense. Open your brain and your heart to others and the world—know your passion and your purpose—and cross the river and burn the boat.

Forgiveness is one of the most powerful forces we human beings possess. We have it at our fingertips 100% of the time. We simply need to consciously choose to act on it.

Decide to wear YOUR red.

Forgive.

Don't look back.

You are not going that way.

NEGATIVITY

Another big roadblock—habit of thought—that gets in the way of our authenticity, success and happiness is negativity.

It can unravel the best of intentions and squelch the most positive of spirits—if we let it and/or if we are unaware of it. Negativity is one of those things that becomes a habit of thought. An unrelenting and destructive attitude. We don't even know we are thinking it. When we view the world through a negative lens, we will see exactly what we expect to see – negativity. We don't have to look very far to find it either. Sadly, it's around us every day and in increasing frequency across the globe. We only need to pick up our cell phone, turn on the computer, watch the news, listen to the radio or be around people to be inundated by all that is wrong with our world and the people in it.

But what would happen if we took in all the bad things with a neutral approach or even a positive approach? I am not talking about being a Pollyanna or donning the rose-colored glasses. We need to be acutely aware of what is happening in our world. However, when we see through a negative lens, we place a lot of filters on those events that exist many times only in our own minds, based on our own unique experiences and influencers.

Talk about getting in our own way! When we 'see' and experience things through a negative, closed mind and a 'sky is falling' mindset, we only get about 10% of the overall potential of that experience. On the other hand, if we flip the switch in our brains to be open minded, creative, welcoming and inquisitive, we reap 100% of the experience. We come away enlightened and with more knowledge and understanding! Here's a simple story to illustrate this point:

Chapter 4 - Cross the River and Burn the Boat

Two young men are traveling around the country looking for a new place to live. They are not traveling together, nor are they aware of each other or know one another. It just so happens that on different days in one week, they each happen upon the same town and meet the same person.

The first young man walked into the town and meandered around the town square, the shops, restaurants and inns. As he turned a corner, he happened onto an old-style hardware store with an elderly gentleman sitting on the porch in a well-worn rocking chair.

The boy walked up to the old man and said, "Hello. I've been traveling the country looking for a nice place to live. This seems like a fine town from what I have seen. What kind of people live here?" The gentlemen responded with a smile, and answered the boy's question with another question. "Well, my boy, what kind of people have you found in all the other towns you have visited so far?"

The boy responded by saying, "None of the other towns have been very friendly. The people were cold and rude, standoffish and downright mean. I didn't see anything or meet anyone that really interested me or that I found engaging in any way." "Well", said the old man, "I'm sorry to tell you that you will find much the same kind of people here."

With that, the young man walked away with his head hanging down, a frown on his face, an exasperated sigh and slump of resignation in his shoulders.

A few days later, the other young man came into the town and walked much the same path around the town square, shops, restaurants and inns as the other boy had done. Sure enough, as he walked around a corner, he saw the same elderly gentlemen on the porch of the old-fashioned hardware store.

He approached the elderly gentleman and said, "Excuse me, sir. My name is Ethan. I've been wondering around this great country looking for a new place to live. Your town here looks so nice! If you wouldn't mind telling me, what kind of people live here?"

With that, the old man smiled and answered the young man's question with a question. "Well, son. I'd be interested to know what kind of people you have found in the other towns you have visited?" And the boy responded with, "Oh my. You see, that's the problem! Everywhere I have been, the people are wonderful! They are warm, welcoming, fun to talk with—some have even invited me to dinner and let me sleep in their barn! It's been an amazing journey so far!"

"Ha", chuckled the old man. "You will find exactly the same kind of people here, my boy! Good luck with your decision!" The boy shook the gentleman's hand, thanked him for the conversation and continued on his way—shoulders squared, a smile on his face and spirit in his step.

With that, the older gentlemen's helper came to the door and stepped outside onto the porch. He looked at the old man and said, "Sam, I don't get it. You have had two boys stop by here in the last week. Both asked you exactly the same question, but you gave each of them a completely different answer. What's up with that?" "Marty, the answer to their question was not to be found in our town. They already had the answer in their head. Their attitude showed up before they arrived in each of the towns they visited. The first boy sees everything and everyone as negative—and that is exactly what he found. The second boy sees everything as positive—and that is exactly what he found. Funny thing about life. You usually get exactly what you think you will get."

And so it is with you. What do expect? What do you think? Be mindful. Whatever you expect and whatever you think—you will get. Self-awareness and recognizing unconscious habits of thoughts are the first steps. Once you know what is going on in your mind—you can change it. And once you do that, the possibilities are endless.

> "NOBODY CAN MAKE YOU FEEL INFERIOR WITHOUT YOUR CONSENT."
>
> **ELEANOR ROOSEVELT**

SELF-CONFIDENCE – IT CAN MAKE OR BREAK YOUR SUCCESS...

Take your internal motivation and new self-awareness of your conditioning and set specific goals to change your thinking and behavior. Even the smallest new awareness and behavior change to the positive will have a big impact on a critical success factor—your self-confidence.

Why do we spend so much time and energy chasing self-confidence? Do you ever find yourself wondering why so many other people seem to possess it effortlessly, and why not you?

The truth is, we all experience moments (and sometimes longer, much longer periods of time) where we have a total lack of self-confidence. The opposite is also true. We all have moments, when we feel invincible and are full of self-confidence! Not ego, but confidence and we are in our zone. We also can be everywhere and anywhere in between this trauma and triumph.

Why?

Behavioral psychologists tell us that self-confidence, or the lack thereof, is how we think and feel about ourselves. And how we think and feel about ourselves is a direct result of our conditioning from when we were growing up, and as we continue on our life journey as adults. Our experiences and those people and things that had influence over us create a significant portion of our self-talk and self-beliefs. What are you saying to yourself? Is it true, or something you simply think is true?

The experiences we go through, the words we hear, the influences we are exposed to all send messages to our brains about who we are and who we are not. We begin to assume we are what and who these messages are telling us we are—how smart, capable, attractive, kind, strong or the opposites of these— and we believe it all to be true. Since we believe these things we then manifest the behavior that supports the belief and voila! We have fulfilled our destiny as predetermined by everything and everyone outside of ourselves have told us!

And we wonder why we end up feeling unhappy and unfilled!

> "IT'S NOT WHO YOU ARE THAT HOLDS YOU BACK, IT'S WHO YOU THINK YOU'RE NOT."
>
> **AUTHOR UNKNOWN**

The voices in our head (both the silent and noisy ones) are convincing us of things that simply are not true. These voices are only repeating what they have been told over and over again by external forces. But be aware this is simply, once again, a human being thing. It's normal! Once we become aware of why we are lacking in self-esteem and confidence, we can then start to do something about it.

So, what do we do and how do we maintain it? We need to take the time to consciously build and support our own self-confidence and that of those around us. Not in a false way, but in a very positive way—based on our strengths with a focus on who we really are and all of the unique strengths and gifts we have to offer. We need to recognize the importance of self-confidence and what we can do to nurture it in ourselves and those around us each and every day.

It sounds trite and overused, but it's true we need to believe. Even when you doubt 'yourself', do it anyway. Of course, prepare for whatever that next 'do it' thing is, but then step up and step out! This is what begins building your self-esteem and self-confidence.

When I left my corporate life to start my business, I was scared—really scared. I had no idea if I was smart enough, brave enough, talented enough to be successful on my own. One of the most important things I knew, however, was that I had to first, define what 'success' was to me—not anyone else.

Once I did, I then wrote a complete and detailed vision of what that success looked like; planned what I needed to do to make it happen; and then took the action to manifest it. Simple? Yes. Easy? Honestly, no. But lo and behold, it happened. And I was so busy dreaming, planning and taking action, I forgot to be afraid, my self-esteem and confidence grew with every win, no matter how small or big, and somewhere along the way I changed. I began to believe in me. And it can happen for you, too.

AFFIRMATIONS

Affirmations help me a lot. Most of us are familiar with the idea of using positive affirmations to further our growth, success and achievements, but few understand how or why affirmations really work, or use them in our lives on a regular basis.

Not everyone believes in using affirmations. And that's OK. Nothing will work if you do not believe in it—including yourself. So here was my first affirmation: "I have the power of positive attraction." Simple, right? But profound to me. I knew that if I could attract positivity (people, circumstances, opportunity and events) into my life, then I would know what do with it and be willing to take action. This worked then and it still does now.

So just what is an affirmation? An affirmation is "telling yourself in times of doubt that which you know to be true at other times."

So how does it work? The human mind is different from those of other living creatures in that it has two unique parts—the subconscious mind, and the conscious mind. These two minds work together to create our thoughts, behavior and actions. The subconscious mind encompasses the stuff of memories, conditioning, the nervous system, emotions, and your most basic underlying attitudes. It continuously sends these thoughts to your conscious mind, where this information is then used to consciously make decisions, determine goals, and gather knowledge for the purpose of taking some kind of action.

> "THE THING ALWAYS HAPPENS THAT YOU REALLY BELIEVE IN; AND THE BELIEF IN A THING MAKES IT HAPPEN."
>
> **FRANK LLOYD WRIGHT**

Your life is a result of your actions. Your actions are a result of your thoughts and attitudes. Those thoughts and attitudes are a direct result of your automatic guidance system and it is either operating as a success mechanism or a failure mechanism.

Are you where you want to be? Is your life the best it can be? Every day, consciously send your subconscious mind positive affirmations of who and where you want to be, as if you are already there. Your mind is an amazing and powerful gift—use it. It will believe what you tell it to believe and help guide you to the life you want to have and to the person you want to be.

> "IF YOU ARE DISTRESSED BY ANYTHING EXTERNAL, THE PAIN IS NOT DUE TO THE THING ITSELF, BUT TO YOUR ESTIMATE OF IT; AND THIS YOU HAVE THE POWER TO REVOKE AT ANY MOMENT."
>
> **MARCUS AURELUIS**

How this translates into building our self-esteem and self-confidence in both the workplace and building our lives and careers is significant.

People with high self-confidence and low ego excel to extraordinary levels. These are the people we want leading

Chapter 4 - Cross the River and Burn the Boat

our teams, working in our companies, living next door and watching our kids. They enjoy helping others to succeed. They communicate their expectations clearly and consistently. They offer positive feedback and ideas to increase individual and team success. They motivate those under their prevue to take action in order to accomplish more.

> "ONLY AS HIGH AS I REACH CAN I GROW,
> ONLY AS FAR AS I SEEK CAN I GO,
> ONLY AS DEEP AS I LOOK CAN I SEE,
> ONLY AS MUCH AS I DREAM CAN I BE."
> **KAREN RAVN**

Self-confidence—and not ego—is critical to every area of success. It's important to recognize low self-confidence in ourselves and others and then work to improve it.

The key is action. Do something.

Whether in your own life and/or in working with others, keep a sharp lookout for signs of low self-confidence and work to make it stronger. Develop self-affirmations. Give yourself 100% permission to be confident! Go ahead. Give it a try! See how it feels. By the way, it's liberating.

With others? Meet, talk. Find out what's going right, and what's not going so right. Determine together what can be done to improve the situation and do it. Create a plan. Inspire momentum.

Believe in you. Your self-confidence—your self-esteem can only come from one source. You.

 **GO FOR GOLD**

Are you a frog on a log?
- Are you just deciding to take action or are you taking action?
- What have you been putting off and not doing? Write it down.
- What action do you need to take NOW? Do it. Jump. Once you do, your self-confidence has started growing a bit!

Be aware of past conditioning.
- What's holding you back that you have not been aware of?
- What are your 'habits of thought' and what motivates you—really gets your energy and enthusiasm going? Gets you in the zone?

What and who do you need to forgive?
- Yourself first, then others. What will it take for you to do this? When will you do it? Write it down.
- Caution, negative thoughts can undermine the best effort and best of intentions. It can sneak up on you, check yourself.
- Are you getting 10% of your life experience or 100%. Why or why not? What do you need to do to get it to 100%?

Believe in yourself.

- Make a list of all the things that you do best in the world. These are unique to you. This is your 0.2mg gold—go for it.

CHAPTER 5

PURPOSE. PASSION. POWER.

> "EFFORTS AND COURAGE ARE NOT ENOUGH WITHOUT PURPOSE AND DIRECTION."
>
> **JOHN F. KENNEDY**

UNDERSTANDING YOUR TRUE PURPOSE, passion and power is a game changer. Finally getting there, however, takes time and reflection.

Consider this...

Does a goldfish on the inside of the bowl see herself the way the people do from the outside of the bowl? No, of course not. Human beings are not any different. We look at ourselves from the inside—a very different perspective than those around us who see us from the outside. So how do we really begin to understand how we are perceived, not how we think we are perceived? By going deep to understand our purpose, passion and power, strengths, challenges, values, thoughts, emotions, experiences and behavior—from our own perspective and that of others who are trusted and see us in action in different circumstances. Only with information and feedback can we begin to understand how our minds work and why, and how this creates obstacles or solutions to our success and happiness.

Chapter 5 - Purpose. Passion. Power.

DEFINE AND FOCUS ON STRENGTHS

> "TO BE WHAT WE ARE, AND TO BECOME WHAT WE ARE CAPABLE OF BECOMING, IS THE ONLY END OF LIFE."
>
> **BARUCH SPINOZA**

Most of us know extremely well what we do not do well. We spent our early education years working on the c's, d's and f's to bring them up to a's and b's, right? I often wonder what would have happened if instead of working on the stuff we didn't do well, we focused on those things in which we excelled? It would be very unrealistic to do this in our early educations because of course, we are discovering our strengths and challenges and the education process allows us to do that through the grading system.

But what about when we get older and we are starting to think about college and career and life's ambitions and desires? Do we still need to spend most of our time working on our opportunities for development, limitations or challenges? If we do, what is happening to our unique talents and gifts?

Parents, teachers and managers generally mean well in pointing out our deficits, and indeed, some areas of learning, development and improvement are critical to our success. But we have become experts in our own weaknesses and spend our lives trying to repair our flaws, while our strengths lie dormant and neglected.

So, why are we so reluctant to focus on our strengths and make them even stronger? Despite your achievements, you may wonder whether you are as talented as everyone thinks you are.

You suspect that luck and circumstance may have played a big part in your getting to where you are today.

My take on this is: we get our poor skills elevated to mediocre—great! And our strongest skills and talents lay ignored and dormant and are certainly not getting any stronger! And where is our happiness quotient when we work on weaknesses? Think this might have something to do with low self-esteem?

Don't misunderstand, it is certainly important to challenge ourselves to up-the-bar in areas where we are not strong and to learn new things that are not necessarily squarely in our wheel house, but it is equally important (if not more important in my view) to know and work on our strengths. What we inherently do well and enjoy doing. This is where the gold is—this where our power and inner champion reside.

> "OUR DEEPEST FEAR IS NOT THAT WE ARE INADEQUATE. OUR DEEPEST FEAR IS THAT WE ARE POWERFUL BEYOND MEASURE…WE ASK OURSELVES, "WHO AM I TO BE BRILLIANT, GORGEOUS, TALENTED, FABULOUS?" ACTUALLY, WHO ARE YOU NOT TO BE? YOUR PLAYING SMALL DOESN'T SERVE THE WORLD."
>
> **MARIANNE WILLIAMSON**

By not focusing on, learning, understanding and nurturing your strengths, you miss out on discovering more of who you really are—who you are truly meant to become. As mentioned in Chapter 1, there is a wonderful tool that I use in all of my coaching and group work: "Strengths Finder 2.0", by the #1 New

York Times bestselling author, Tom Rath. Here is an excerpt from Tom's introduction to the book and the assessment:

"*In 1998, I began working with a team of Gallup scientists led by the late Father of Strengths Psychology, Donald O. Clifton. Our goal was to start a global conversation about what's right with people.*

We were tired of living in a world that revolved around fixing our weaknesses. Society's relentless focus on people's shortcomings had turned into a global obsession. What's more, we had discovered that people have several times more potential for growth when they invest energy in developing strengths instead of correcting their deficiencies.

Based on Gallup's 40-year study of human strengths, we created a language of the 34 most common talents and developed the Clifton StrengthsFinder assessment to help people discover and describe these talents.

...our studies indicate that people who [do] have the opportunity to focus on their strengths every day are <u>six times as likely to be engaged in their jobs</u> and more than <u>three times as likely to report having an excellent quality of life in general</u>."

On January 13, 2016, Gallup.com released a study on employee engagement that was done in 2015. Here are just a few of the results that were a result of the study:

EMPLOYEE ENGAGEMENT IN U.S. STAGNANT IN 2015

PERCENTAGE OF EMPLOYEES ENGAGED IN U.S.

2014	2015
31.5%	32.0%

GALLUP DAILY TRACKING

by Amy Adkins

Story Highlights

- 32% of U.S. employees engaged in 2015
- Monthly averages largely consistent
- Engagement flat since 2000

WASHINGTON, D.C. -- The percentage of U.S. workers in 2015 who Gallup considered engaged in their jobs averaged 32%. The majority (50.8%) of employees were "not engaged," while another 17.2% were "actively disengaged." The 2015 averages are largely on par with the 2014 averages and reflect little improvement in employee engagement over the past year.

The 2015 employee engagement average is based on Gallup Daily tracking interviews conducted with 80,844 adults working for an employer. Gallup categorizes workers as "engaged" based on their ratings of key workplace elements—such as having an opportunity to do what they do best each day, having someone at work who encourages their development and believing their *opinions count at work—that predict important organizational performance outcomes.*

U.S. Employee Engagement, 2011-2015
Yearly averages

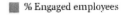
% Engaged employees

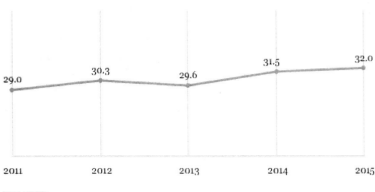

GALLUP

Engaged employees are involved in, enthusiastic about and committed to their work. Gallup's extensive research shows that employee engagement is strongly connected to business outcomes essential to an organization's financial success, such as productivity, profitability and customer engagement. Engaged employees support the innovation, growth and revenue that their companies need.

And this is just one of a multitude of studies that show the importance of working in our strengths if we want to be engaged in our careers and in our lives and make a real difference.

It's a challenging way to think for most of us. We have been conditioned, trained, to work on overcoming our weaknesses and shortcomings. And for most of us, I would guess this has all been in our best interests. But just imagine if we flipped this over, became aware of we what do best, and then went out actually did it!

It takes courage to face up to your strengths and talents. Once you do, you are then accountable. It's much easier to fall back and just work on the things you don't do well. That way, no one can really be all that critical about your performance, behavior and results. After all, there is only way to go when you are at the bottom. Up. So, good for you.

Not really.

Challenge yourself instead! Really think about what you do extremely well – what you would love to do more of and what you would love to do less of and then learn how to do both more often! This is not about finding a way out of work. It IS about finding a way to work in your talents and have the work not be work at all! You will work harder, longer and more successfully – and you will enjoy every moment from the get-go.

Once you do make the flip to your strengths, remember—you are now aware. You are now accountable for being the best YOU, you can be; live up to yourself. You will become more true, more genuine and more authentically you.

20 MILLION DOLLARS

Finding our strengths usually has something to do with our passion. The two are inherently entwined. In addition to knowing our strengths, it is equally important to know what is behind those strengths—what is the passion that is driving our strengths?

Some time ago, I was working on a leadership development program for a client and was looking for a good exercise or example to use that would bring this idea of finding passion home to the group. I also wanted to attach it to real life issues so it would be clear and personal for each of the individuals in the group.

In my search, I happened upon a terrific video done by Brian Tracy. He is the Chairman and CEO of Brian Tracy International and is one of the most well-known, successful and respected professionals in the training and development fields in the world today. You can learn more about Brian on his website at <u>www.briantracy.com</u>.

He offers a vast resource of books, videos and materials in many different areas of personal and professional development and I just love soaking in all of his insights and guidance, as well as that of many other leadership gurus, past and present.

One of the thousands of great videos Brian has made and shared with the world is called "Organizing Your Life". In this video, he challenges us to think about what is really important to us—what are our true priorities—and what drives us to stay focused on them and achieve our goals. This is an exercise that is used at Stanford University by the business faculty to promote creative thinking and clarity. It's called the 20/10 exercise.

It goes like this:

You have inherited twenty million dollars free and clear. At the same time, however, you have been told that due to a medical condition, you only have 10 more years to live.

There are two important questions you now have to ask yourself:

1. *Who am I, really?*
2. *What do I want from life?*

Chapter 5 - Purpose. Passion. Power.

You have all the money you will ever need. There are no limitations on your time (except the 10 years) or talent – so what will you do? What choices will you make?

Write it down. This is very revealing on a very personal and professional level.

Based on this, write down 10 goals that you want to achieve in the next 12 months. If you could only accomplish just one of these goals—which one would it be? Which one will have the greatest positive impact on your life?

Make that the sole purpose of all of your decisions and actions. This is at the root of your purpose and passion.

This is a great exercise to do several times a year just to stay on track and focused on what is most important to you, the life you want to live and the legacy you want to leave.

"A PROBLEM UNSOLVED IS MERELY A GOAL UNACHIEVED."

BRIAN TRACY

THE BLACK LINE – OR – LOCATION, LOCATION, LOCATION

Created with Kaley Warner Klemp

There is another great organization called The Conscious Leadership Group*. They have the most incredible, animated ways of explaining how we get in our own way of happiness and success. My favorite is a video they created called, "Location, Location, Location." It's all about a black line and whether or not we are above it or below it in every moment.

Our location determines how we respond and behave in any given situation and in any given moment. You can download the video and the PDF from their website at *http://conscious.is/video/locating-yourself-a-key-to-conscious-leadership* . In the meantime, here is the overview of the BLACK LINE:

The Conscious Leadership Group explains that we are always either above or below the black line.

Above the line is a "by me" state. It means we are in a state of openness, creativity, confidence, collaboration, presence, curiosity, growth and learning. We are in a state of acceptance and trust. Our beliefs are well-grounded, our behaviors reflect our beliefs, and the statements—the words we use—are positive and unarguable.

Below the line, however, is a "to me" state. It means we are in a state of drama, defensiveness, scarcity, resistance and toxic fear. And, our beliefs are grounded in being right, needing approval, being afraid and our behaviors reflect these beliefs, and our statements—the words we use—are negative and rigid.

ABOVE THE LINE

Beliefs	Behaviors	Statements
• Its more valuable to learn and grow than be right • There are more than two possibilities • Approval, control and security are something I already have • It is valuable to question my thoughts and beliefs • From a distance, nothing is serious and most everything is funny • All people and circumstances are my allies • Revealing is more valuable than concealing	• Breathe • Significantly change my posture • Get curious • Listen consciously • Feel emotions • Speak unarguably • Appreciate • Take responsibility • Question my beliefs • Recognize unconscious beliefs • Create win for all solutions • Play • Make impeccable agreements	• What can I learn from this? • How is the opposite as true? • How is this familiar? • I appreciate you for… • I take responsibility for… • I agree to… • I choose to… • I create… • This isn't serious • What I hear you saying… • My body sensations are… • I feel (sad, angry, scared, joyful)

Above the Line (BY ME) Presence/Curiosity/Growth & Learning Acceptance and Trust

Below the Line (TO ME) Drama/Defensiveness/Scarcity Resistance & Toxic Fear

Beliefs	Behaviors	Statements
• Being right is the most important thing • There is a threat to me occurring out there • There is not enough • I need another's approval • Safety and security come from outside myself • I need to be in control (of things I cannot control) • One side of polarity is better than the other • There are only two options • This serious (it is not funny) • I am better than/ less than • There is a right/ wrong way • There is no choice • My story is true	• Cling to an opinion • Find fault/blame • Fight/flee/ freeze/faint • Argue • Rationalize/ Justify • See others as needing help • Gossip • Get overwhelmed • Do whatever it takes to defend/ guarantee the survival of my identity • Use distractions to relieve pain (food, sex, drugs, media, work) • Enroll others to affirm my beliefs • Avoid all disconfirming data • Attack the messenger • Avoid conflict • Force everything into polarity (right/wrong, good/bad)	• I should • I can't • I'm right • It's hard • I'm trying • It's not my fault • I'm confused • The "fact" is • I have to • You made me • I'm sorry (with an excuse) • Always/never • "Why" questions • You are not listening to me • It's no use • My way or the highway • They don't get it

Really take some time and think about your beliefs, behaviors and statements. Where are you most of the time? Above or below the line? What kind of results are you getting when you are in each place?

Awareness, conscious awareness, of where we are in any given circumstance can mean the difference between good and bad choices, behaviors and actions. All of which impact the results we get and where we end up. Above the line is the best location—every time.

Above the line is where we are centered in our best selves in our own personal power.

Personal Power Vs Authority

> "LEADERSHIP IS THE ART OF GETTING SOMEONE ELSE TO DO SOMETHING YOU WANT DONE—BECAUSE THEY WANT TO DO IT."
>
> **Dwight D. Eisenhower**

Power

What is your level of personal power? It's a sign of authentic leadership and an important quality to develop in life and in business. There is a big difference between personal power and granted authority, however, many people have the tendency to use the words interchangeably.

These words refer to two very different aspects of leadership. Let me tell you how I stumbled into learning the difference between the two...

Before I went to work for the company I told you about earlier—

the one that was taken over by the corporate behemoth—I had been working in South Florida for a small boutique consulting firm. It was a great company with great people, but I just could not find my unique niche and intellectual and creative freedom with them. That, combined with the fact that I was absolutely, positively miserable in Florida—between the heat, humidity, relentless sun and ever increasing population and crowding—I reached a point where I could not get out of there fast enough.

I thought for long time about where I wanted to go and what I wanted to do next. The what I wanted to do next was still in question, but I had decided to move to the East Coast. I have always, and still do, love New England. Now I had a chance to experience it for myself. So, I moved to Connecticut and began a job search.

On a lark, I answered an ad for an Executive Assistant to the President of a small manufacturing company. I had no intention of taking a job like this, but I was curious about the company, what they did, and wanted to get as much interviewing experience as I could to polish and strengthen my skills. So, at the first interview I met and talked with the three primary owners of the company—the President, Vice President of Sales and the Financial Officer. (Many years later, I would refer to these three gentlemen as the Lion, the Scarecrow and the Tin Man—I was, of course, Dorothy.) These three men were at the helm of a specialty resin company that manufactured unique and high-end coating systems for commercial and industrial floors—both new and retrofits.

After a series of interviews, they offered me the job, but then I turned them down. I did not want to be anyone's secretary and I would be lousy at it anyway. So instead, I offered to work for them for 90 days and during that time spend time in every department, division and activity that I could to understand and learn their business. At the end of the 90 days, I would give them a report of my experience and thoughts about moving forward together—or not—and we could either come to an agreement on my position, or part friends and move in a different direction. They agreed!

And so, I began my 90-day adventure. I swept floors, worked in the lab, made and packed samples, went on sales calls, got a hard hat and steel-toed boots to visit construction sites and clients, learned to drive a forklift, sat with the finance people, the shipping people, the executives and the admins, and played some golf with the boys, and I came to understand what a special company this was and what a great group of people worked there. I also saw the potential of what the company could become. I wanted to be a part of it. I did not want to be a secretary.

I came back with my 90-day report on what I had seen, learned and experienced and offered a very in-depth proposal for how we could move forward together, if we could reach an agreement. This proposal was incredibly detailed in terms of what I saw as a strategy for the business and a change in thinking and behavior about what the company did, in brief: the company needed to shift from a product focus to a relationship focus. And I offered to lead the change. We had a long discussion and I was delighted that each of these three men took all of this very seriously, asked a lot of good questions and eventually came to the consensus that we should move forward together.

We worked out the details of our agreement and then came the final two decisions for me to make:

Chapter 5 - Purpose. Passion. Power.

1. My title
2. My salary

I told them I wanted my title to be Queen, but if that was not acceptable, then I would run with Director, for now. They agreed to Director.

They wrote a number on a piece of paper as the salary. I looked at it. Drew a line through it. Wrote a different number. They smiled. We agreed to my number.

With that we all stood up, shook hands and made plans for dinner later that evening. WOW. Talk about being in the zone of personal power! That was the start of my 12-year career with the with this company and where I learned the difference between power and authority.

Without realizing what I was doing, I was tapping into my innermost power. For maybe the first time in my life, I was not trying to morph myself into something others wanted me to be or thought I should be—instead, I instinctively looked at this opportunity and started designing, creating, imagining, crafting what it COULD be in an ideal world, in MY ideal world, that would also benefit the company and its people beyond anything they had imagined!

I created my destiny. And in doing so, the energy and power that fueled this passion carried over into the three men that owned the company and influenced them to see the possibilities and to buy into it in a big way.

My relationships with these three men was one of great respect, trust and fellowship—I never really reported to any of them—we all worked together and supported each other in all of our strengths and weaknesses. Title and authority did not play here; personal power did.

As I have thought about it all these years later, I realize that I have continued this approach in everything I have done since and it has been liberating. That's not to say it's been easy—quite the contrary. But in my experience, anything worth having (especially freedom, independence and living life in your own way) is never easy, but it is more than worth the effort.

It boils down to this—simply put, power is the inner passion and authenticity of purpose that provides us the capacity, the ability, to influence the attitudes and behavior of others. It is not about title, rank, position or authority. It is simply the ability to motivate yourself and others to take specific actions because you and they want to.

Authority on the other hand, is the right granted from a person or an organization to another to represent, or to act, in a specified way. For example, the CEO of a company is given the authority by the board of directors to run the company. In turn, the CEO places managers in positions of authority over the various divisions and departments of the organization.

Authority is granted, but always has defined limits. Power is earned—and can be limitless. Most of us know that a person can possess a great deal of power and no authority. Conversely, a person can have authority, but absolutely no power.

Real, genuine, authentic power creates a climate of trust, cooperation, and accomplishment in which people are positively motivated to pursue their own goals and the goals of the organization.

So, what is your level of personal power? Whatever it may be, you can continue to build on it by simply being you—genuinely you. Be intentional about shaping your life according to your values and priorities. Don't morph yourself into someone others are telling you to be. Trust yourself. Believe in yourself. Be honest with yourself. When you do, others will trust, believe and be honest with you, and this is the foundation that enhances personal power.

 **GO FOR GOLD**

What are your strengths?
- Take some self-assessments to determine and/or affirm your inherent talents and strengths.
- Write them down and then ask yourself if you are primarily working in the areas of strengths or not. If not, what can you do to spend more time in your strengths?

What would you do with 20 million dollars and 10 years to live?
- This may seem silly, but it is not. Write down your plan for the next 10 years of your life and how you would use that 20 million. This is a great way to understand your priorities and make a plan around them.

Are you above or below the line?
- Why?
- Why not?

What is your source of personal power?

- Look at opportunities from outside the lines. Be creative, courageous and imaginative!
- What opportunities do you have right now—right in front of you that you are not seeing—that you can create into a wonderful adventure, journey and success in either or both of your personal and professional lives? Step up and step out.

PART II

IGNITE

THE FIRST 'i' IN i3 is ***inspire.*** This is your vision, dream, passion for doing, becoming, evolving. These are critically important to leading your best life and becoming all that you can be. Writing these things down and thinking about them intentionally and purposefully is essential to actually manifesting them into reality. But all that being said, it still is not enough. We must have a workable plan and a plan that works.

Now we move on to the second 'i' – ***ignite.***

As mentioned earlier, most of us spend more time planning a vacation than we do planning our lives! Think about it. When you plan a vacation, you usually start with a destination in mind— where you desire to go. Right? Good! You have a vision! Now, you start thinking about all the things you would like to do when you get there, right? Let's imagine that this particular vacation is a winter get-a-way to a tropical island for 10 days. Yum, sounds wonderful! So, we pick the island and then start thinking about everything we want to do once we get there; snorkeling, swimming, sight-seeing, tennis, sunset cruise, dinners, and the list goes on. By now, you have your tablet (pen and paper or electronic) out and you are making a list and researching all the things that interest you and the resorts and hotels that suit you.

Oh, and of course you need to plan your budget, how you will get there- plane, train, automobile, when will you leave and when will you return, what to pack, what needs to be done before you leave—stop the mail and the paper and alert the neighbors to keep an eye on the house, Fido's reservation at the Pet Lodge, and the list goes on and on until you have every detail meticulously planned, timed, and an action plan to make it all happen.

Congratulations! You have just completed a thorough strategic plan! And no doubt it will be an enormously wonderful vacation. Why? Because you planned it that way.

Is your life any different? Not really. And yet, how many of us actually take the time to create a life plan? One that is ours—with a desired destination—one that stirs our excitement, joy, anticipation and that we own. Not too many of us. Instead, we react to the world around us and make decisions and go in the direction of what is happening to us—instead of thinking, planning and deciding how we will happen upon the world. It takes courage to happen and not be happened to, but the difference between the two is either reacting to life or creating a life—which one do you want?

You have started thinking and working on your vision; or perhaps you have already defined it. Bravo. But here's the deal:

Einstein told us that if we continue to do the same thing and expect a different result—what are we? Insane. If you want to create different outcomes in your life, then you must start to do things differently. And this is one of the hardest things human beings are faced with—change. Being and doing differently starts with thinking differently, and consciously and intentionally behaving differently. Reinvention of self. I think I am currently on about the 6th or 7th reinvention of myself—and each one is more and more fascinating to me—and the best part is, I like myself more with each iteration. Experience is indeed a great teacher, but only if we are asking "what can I learn?"

How do you want to reinvent YOU?

CHAPTER 6

REINVENT

> "GLAM REALLY DID PLANT SEEDS FOR A NEW IDENTITY. I THINK A LOT OF KIDS NEEDED THAT—THAT SENSE OF REINVENTION. KIDS LEARNED THAT HOWEVER CRAZY YOU MAY THINK IT IS, THERE IS A PLACE FOR WHAT YOU WANT TO DO AND WHO YOU WANT TO BE."
>
> **DAVID BOWIE**

Once we have done a deep self-reflection and gathered feedback and information on what we as individuals do best in the world—then and only then do we begin to see a clear vision of who and what we can and want to become. Now you have that vision, you SEE it! Feeling exhilarated? You should be! This is powerful stuff. But don't be the frog and just decide, now you must take action!

Ignite your vision!

And there is a formula for actualizing your vision. Roll up your sleeves. Now the heavy lifting begins—let's begin pouring the foundation and igniting your i3 plan.

THE FORMULA

After the corporate journey had come to a close, and I realized what I wanted to do—I needed to reinvent in a big way. I needed education and training that I could marry to my experience, skills and talents and then take it forward into the world.

I did an exhaustive search for organizations, schools and other educational and training entities where I could engage and learn in a deep understanding of leadership and how to bring it to other people and organizations. As a life-long learner, this was—and continues to be—one of the best parts of what I do!

In my work, association and initial leadership credentialing with Resource Associates Corporation in Reading, PA, one of the first things I learned was the power of this formula. It is called the "Formula for Success." Here it is:

$$A + (s \& k) + G = PBC \quad I/R$$

Start from the right and read to the left.

I/R – what is this? It stands for "improved results." Why, you may ask. Because if we narrow all of this self-development, leadership, vision, goals, planning et al into one thing—one common denominator that encapsulates what we are trying to achieve, it would be to improve our results on myriad of different personal and professional levels.

Make sense? If it does, then the next question we need to ask is, "OK, so if the end result is improved results, what do we have to DO to make that happen?"

Let me answer that question with a question. If we continue to do the same things in the same way and expect a different result—what are we? As I said before, Einstein would tell us we are insane, and he would be right.

So, if we want a different result—an improved result—we need do things differently and better.

PBC—Positive Behavior Change. We need to change our behavior in order to change our results. All of everything we do, achieve, do not do, and do not achieve is based on our behavior.

This begs the question, "What is behavior and how do I change it?" Behavior is action—the things we do—the way we behave. Our behavior is what other people observe about us and, sad as it may be, draw conclusions and make judgements about us on both a personal and professional level. They are making decisions about us—our leadership, integrity, intelligence, upbringing, attitudes and so forth—based on our behavior! And most of the time, we are not even aware of our behavior let alone how it is affecting others!

So, we need to become much more self-aware and recognize both our positive and negative behavior. And then make a conscious effort to make Positive Behavior Change!

Ok—so now we know we need to change, but how? What do we need to make the kind of changes we want to make?

That's where the **G** and the **(s & k)** part of the formula kick in. Any idea what the G is?

GOALS. Without goals, we have no direction, no purpose and no way of knowing what we are achieving and when. Not only do we need goals, they MUST be written! I have a writer friend who told me one time, "Nothing is real until it is written."

I always ask the groups and individuals I work with if they have goals. The answer is always is yes 100% of the time. Then I ask how many have their goals written down. The percentage drops to at least 50% if not less. If you do not have your goals written down, they are not goals. They are just ideas that are floating around in your head and will fall off the radar as soon as the next hair-on-fire situation comes up, someone bursts into your office with an issue, your cell phone rings, or any number of other things that happen every day. The point is—make a habit of setting goals and writing them down! We will go into more detail on how to create a goal setting and achieving process that actually works in the next chapter.

So now we have the GOAL part of the formula ready to go—what is the (s & k)?

Skills and Knowledge. We all have skills and knowledge in abundance. We have been taught things all of our lives from our parents, care givers, teachers, clergy, friends, family, associates, colleagues, mentors, bosses and others. Don't underestimate your knowledge or skills—you probably have much more of both than you realize, we all do. The problem is we just don't see it in ourselves. We see it clearly in others and often times feel less because of it. Stop it. YOU are uniquely YOU. And you have a combination of unique gifts of skill, experience, talent and knowledge that are yours and yours and alone. Don't ever let anyone tell you any differently!

So, with all your skills and knowledge, written goals, self-awareness and positive behavior changes taking place, you should already be in that space of I/R—improved results—right?

Maybe. You may be on your way to the I/R, but how far will you really get and is it sustainable? How many times have you gone to a seminar, workshop or some other learning event and come back with a tote bag and a head full of great ideas and new things to try. And then you get inundated by all the stuff of everyday life and business. What happens to all that new S & K and goals? They usually vanish within a few days or weeks.

Why?

Because the most important part of the formula is missing. Remember when we talked about motivation and conditioning in the previous chapter? Well, it plays big time when it comes to the final ingredient in the formula, **A**.

Attitude. What is an attitude? Simply put, it's a thought without thinking. It is something we are not even aware of and yet, it has incredible power over us. Where does it come from—how does it manifest itself in our brains—and why can it have such a negative impact on our success, happiness and becoming the best of who we are? Hmmm... answers to these questions in just a minute. First, a story.

As mentioned earlier, the title of this book has a great deal of meaning—and not just for me, but for anyone who has been told they: "cannot," "should not," "will never be," "are not good enough," "should settle," etc. Whatever your "never wear red" statement was or is in your life, when we hear it enough and from different sources and people over and over again it becomes a truth. We believe it to be true without a doubt. It manifests in our brains and becomes a **habit of thought**. A thought we think without thinking.

Let's pause for a moment and take a closer look at these habits of thought and how they manifest themselves and impact our lives and our world. This is where prejudice begins.

Diversity and inclusion are the current buzz words today. Everyone is suddenly on fire about addressing these issues and formulating processes and systems to incorporate diversity and inclusion in our businesses, schools, communities, cities, politics and the world.

But processes and systems cannot do this. Only people can. And before people can do this they need to understand the root cause – it's attitude. It is within us – not outside of us. Here's why...

An attitude.

This attitude rests in the subconscious brain—we don't pay any attention to it—it's just there, waiting to step up and drive our conscious thoughts, and conscious thoughts drive our behavior, and behavior creates a result: negative or positive, productive or limiting, taking us forward or moving us backward, all without us even knowing we are doing it. WE are the only ones responsible for our lives, outcomes, successes, failures, happiness, joy, just one person—ourselves.

Regardless of what color, nationality, heritage, how we grew up; how much education we have; what position we hold; what gender we are; what our sexual preferences are; etc. - no matter who we are – we have prejudices. Attitudes have developed in our brains through conditioning and we are not even aware of them. This is a human condition. Until we recognize these habits of thoughts for what they are and make a conscious decision to change our thinking, we risk adding to the problems of prejudice and the lack of inclusion and diversity in our society instead of diffusing them.

We need to change our thinking to change our world. We need to develop **cultures** of inclusion and diversity, one person at a time.

Chapter 6 - Reinvent

THE GANG & THE NUN

When I was with the corporation, I traveled extensively all over the world. It was a wonderful experience and I will always be grateful for the adventure, all I learned and all the intriguing places and people I visited and met along the way.

One of my travel adventures, however, stands out as one of the most profound in terms of a huge leap in my own self-awareness and the power of thought and attitude.

This particular trip was domestic. I was living in Woodbury, Connecticut at the time and had made plans to participate in a three-day conference in New York City. Rather than fight the city traffic, I decided to take the train into the city and then back again.

I had not made this trip from Woodbury before, so since there was no train station in Woodbury, I had to drive to Danbury, Connecticut, park the car and then take the train into Grand Central. No problem. It all went perfectly and I enjoyed the ride.

The conference was great and I was looking forward a leisurely ride home at the end of the last day. I arrived at Grand Central on time, found my way to my train back to Danbury, and settled in. Little did I know that the return train was not a direct trip – it stopped in Bridgeport, Connecticut and I had to change trains for the rest of the ride to Danbury.

Now it's important to note that at that time, Bridgeport was one of those towns that had the reputation of being not only unsavory, but downright dangerous for even the most savvy and street-wise people.

We arrived in Bridgeport at around 5:30 PM – it was late Autumn so it was almost dark on the East Coast. Everyone

Chapter 6 - Reinvent

departed the train and except for me – went to the parking lot next to the station, got in their cars and left. I was the only one remaining on the train station platform. Again, not a problem – the connecting train was supposed to be there within 30 minutes, so I would just wait for it and be on my way. By the way, we did not have cell phones at this stage in our technological evolution.

I waited. And waited. And waited. No train. About an hour in, I suddenly noticed a train pulling out from BELOW the station platform and heading north. It was my train. I had no idea there was a lower level where the connector came in – and it had just left without me.

I was stranded. In Bridgeport, Connecticut. In the dark. With no idea where to go or what to do. So, I gathered my wits and started walking off the platform into the parking lot in hopes of finding a store or gas station open where I could call for a cab or bus or something to get me back to Danbury.

As I started across the parking lot, I saw a group of what looked to be young men, walking in my direction. There were about 7 of them. They were black. They were dressed in the 'hood' garb of the day. They had the 'swagger'. I was terrified.

Here was this white girl in her high heels, suit, briefcase and roller bag in an isolated parking lot all alone and in the dark with a gang of black boys eyeing her and 'walkin' the walk' in her direction... with intent. My brain immediately went to all the horror stories – both real and imagined – about what happens in situations like this.

And then, I stopped. I totally changed the scenario in my mind – and thought – what if these boys are not about anything bad, but instead have shown up to help me? Why do I think they

Chapter 6 - Reinvent

are bad? Because of what color they are? How they are dressed? The way they walk? I wrapped my head around this, squared my shoulders, put a smile on my face and with a confidence I really didn't feel, I walked directly toward them and into the middle of the gang.

They surrounded me. I reached up to the meanest-looking, tallest and roughest boy among them and gently but firmly put my hand on his shirt collar and pulled his face towards mine and said with a smile, "Thank God you fellows you showed up! You are my heroes tonight! I am stranded and have no idea how to get out of here and get home – and all of you just appeared! Thank you with all my heart – so where are we going to find a cab?"

A long pause... and then - they smiled back. They started asking how I ended up in the parking lot – how dangerous this was for me and that they were glad to help. They walked around, in front and behind me and escorted me to a limo/cab company a few blocks away. They stayed with me the entire time until I was safely inside the cab and on my way home. I gave them all the money I had in my wallet on the promise they would do something good with it for themselves or others and they promised they would – and I believed them.

I will never forget that evening. I will never forget what my 'attitude' told me and how I changed it into a different a thought and a self-directed outcome. The power of our own thoughts can manifest outcomes. The power of our beliefs can change people's lives. The power of meeting people where they are – letting go of our biases, prejudices and negative attitudes towards ourselves and others, seeing beyond the physical into the heart – can change lives, save lives – and create CULTURES of inclusion and diversity. This is where it begins – inside each of us.

The next time you think you know who another person is or what their story or intention may be – stop. Ask yourself why. Let go of what you think – and open yourself to what IS.

On another, very different occasion, when I was in the fourth grade at St. Michaels school, I had one of my first encounters with the sting of prejudice pointed directly at me.

One of the nuns, Sister Lydia, had it in for me – she hated my red hair, my spunk and me. She seemed hell bent to always find me doing something wrong or against the rules. She was in charge of the all-student Christmas program. She would gather the entire student body into the auditorium once a week for about six weeks prior to the program so we could learn our parts and rehearse the Christmas Carols we would perform for our families and the community.

This was THE event of the year and one that I looked forward to all year. I LOVED this entire process and being part of this wonderful holiday celebration. So this particular year, my fourth-grade year, the day of our first rehearsal had arrived! I could hardly contain myself I was so excited!

The entire student body had gathered in the auditorium and Sister Lydia stood in the center of the stage to begin giving us our instructions for the day. One of the first things she said was that we would start with the Christmas Carols. She would play them one by one and then we would sing and start breaking out into different vocal sections. The one iron clad rule she had was that we were not to sing when she first played the Carol, but to wait until it had played all the way through. And then we would sing as a group as she walked around and starting sorting out the voices.

Of course, I knew the words to every Christmas Carol, so getting started on this part of our program was just the best for me! As she started playing the first Carol, everyone was silent—including me. I made the mistake, however, of moving my lips with the words, no sound came out my mouth not a peep, but my mouth did move.

Talk about a slow pitch.

She hit it out of the park. She abruptly stopped the music in the middle of the Carol. She was still standing center stage. She then said in the loudest voice she had—which by the way was pretty phenomenally loud—"Roxanne Marie Kaufman, march yourself to this stage - immediately!"

I was stunned and had no idea what was going on or what I had done! She then came pounding off the stage and down the aisle, grabbed me by my ear, and dragged me up onto the stage. Center stage.

She stepped to the side and shouted out to the entire student body and faculty "Roxanne Marie Kaufman, your name is MUD! How dare you disrespect my instructions. You are not worthy to be among the students for the Christmas program. You should be utterly ashamed of yourself. Go back to your seat. Do not move your mouth or utter one sound. Do not participate in any way. When our rehearsal is complete, you and I will go to the Principal's office and you will be given your punishment which may include suspension or being expelled."

Needless to say, I was devastated.

She tried to suspend me for 3 days. I was eventually exonerated of all wrong doing. Although I never got an apology in front of the student body, I did get to participate in the Christmas program—but it was never the same again. We moved again the next year and I went to a different school, but I never forgot how that felt.

I share these stories because there are certain things in life that imprint on our brains in rather significant ways that we may not even be aware of and they create these habits of thought—towards others and ourselves that show up as self-defeating pitfalls. Not only do we receive them, we unwittingly give them, as well.

They infiltrate our subconscious brains telling us we are not good enough, not worthy enough, not deserving enough. We think the same thing about others based on what they look like or sound like. For years after St. Michael's school was a distant memory, I could still hear Sister Lydia's voice in my head any time someone questioned my ideas, my choices, my abilities—my name was mud. I knew better in my heart, but the words delivered a powerful punch to my brain.

And I will never forget that gang in Bridgeport – and how they saved me that night – because we all thought differently in that moment.

What voices are you hearing? What voice have you given? How can you change the voices going forward?

Once you begin to understand where these attitudes originate, you can begin to overcome the barriers they create. But first, you must be willing to take a very deep, long look at yourself and where you have been, where you are where you want to go. Then, you begin to get clarity. Then, you begin to see what is in your way .... and it is often an attitude that developed very early on. Once you become aware, you can either eliminate it, change it, go through it, go around it, over it or under it—and begin to make your life and thoughts your own. And pay it forward.

Start making a plan NOW to own your life and your attitudes in your way, in your time. Dig out that 0.2 mg of gold in your heart.

 **GO FOR GOLD**

- Think about what you want to change, improve, eliminate or add to your life to make it 100% your own. Remember, it takes courage and heart to do this. But you have it within you—you just have to tap into it.
- Behaviorial psychologists tell us that 95% of our values and beliefs are formed before we the age of five years old. These values and beliefs form our attitudes. Attitudes drive our thoughts. Our thoughts drive our behavior. What behaviors do you want to change? What thoughts do you need to change to make that happen? What are the hidden attitudes behind those thoughts? Where did they come from? Write all of this down and make a promise to yourself to ferret out those unconscious attitudes that are in your way of creating the success and happiness you envision.
- Make a plan. Now.

CHAPTER 7

LEADERSHIP & STRATEGY

> "I BELIEVE THAT PEOPLE MAKE THEIR OWN LUCK BY GREAT PREPARATION AND GOOD STRATEGY."
>
> **JACK CANFIELD**

We've been talking about many of the things that form our attitudes, thoughts and behavior. These are the things that have gotten us to where we are today—for all the good, bad and everything in between.

All of this is about leadership. Leadership of self. This must always come before any other kind of leadership! So how do we move forward to up the bar on our own self-leadership, who we are and who we want to become? Let's set some framework around what leadership is and what it is not—and look at it from a very practical point of view.

WHAT IS LEADERSHIP AND HOW DO I GET SOME?

As we know, leadership is a word commonly used in reference to formal leadership—corporate teams, individuals in positions of authority, and for those who guide, direct and well, lead. But the word also refers to those who are not formal leaders, those in community service, a leading contender, a mentor, a peer, someone leading a full life.

The capacity for leadership exists within each one of us. But it is up to us to discover it and unleash it! So how do we do it? What is leadership when it is applied to so many different people, in so many different ways?

The answer is found in knowing where leadership begins—personal leadership—leadership of self-first. All formal leadership begins here.

Personal leadership begins with knowing yourself and the direction you want your life to take. The ability to define what you want out of life and how you're going to get it is the first step in developing personal leadership.

> "LEADERSHIP IS PRACTICED NOT SO MUCH IN WORDS AS IN ATTITUDE AND IN ACTIONS".
>
> **HAROLD GENEEN**

Personal leadership then, is 100% accountability for oneself.

When you accept the responsibility and accountability of your own personal leadership, you will begin to realize that you, not others, are responsible for your life. You alone are responsible for your attitudes, actions, and the rewards and consequences of both. You determine the course of your destiny and become the master of your life. You gain the kind of self-confidence that drives the successful outcome of any goal you set for yourself.

This kind of confidence, determination and solution-oriented thinking and action is the foundation of personal, self-leadership that develops our formal leadership—and determines our influence and impact on others—it is leadership by example.

Think for a moment of all the situations in which you are looked to as a leader, either formally or informally, with your children, friends, peers, co-workers, customers, organizations, and ask yourself, "What leadership example am I setting?"

> "IF YOUR ACTIONS INSPIRE OTHERS TO DREAM MORE, LEARN MORE, DO MORE & BECOME MORE, YOU ARE A LEADER."
>
> **JOHN QUINCY ADAMS**

THIS BEGS THE QUESTION, THEN... ARE LEADERS BORN OR MADE?

All leaders are born. But not all who are born are leaders.

Think about someone—past or present—that represents a leader to you.

What specific personality traits does this person possess? How does this person relate to others, professionally and personally? How do they communicate? What is their personal brand? Are they honest, trustworthy, genuine? Do you know their values, principles and vision? Are they consistent in what they say and do?

Do they challenge, innovate and look for new ways to do things? Are they caring, compassionate and real?

Now, ask yourself one more question: Was this leader born with these well-developed leadership traits?

No. No one is.

The characteristics of leadership are learned and developed—they are all qualities and skills that can be improved and honed. It all starts with that gold in our hearts.

The capacity for leadership exists in everyone, but most people never take the time to develop it. A leader combines the vision and curiosity of a dreamer - with the practical engineering of a builder.

A leader knows their own strengths and challenges and is goal directed, looking forward with anticipation toward the attainment of measurable outcomes.

A leader is a person who communicates, interacts and manages self and others with integrity, openness, trust and vision.

A leader sets goals and achieves results.

Motivation, attitude, alignment to strengths and goals give an effective leader meaning and purpose, and serve as a continuous source of success and achievement in pursuit of organizational, team and individual success.

Expect the very best from yourself, for the degree to which you succeed in all aspects of your life lies in your hands. You are the pilot of your own ship and the architect of your future. Your ability to lead both yourself and others will enhance the quality of your work as well as your life.

Self-leadership is the ability to establish a specific direction for your own life, and to proceed in that direction with the self-confidence that comes only to one who knows where he or she is going. Becoming a leader means becoming you. It begins with figuring out who you are, and what gives your life value and meaning.

> "FAR BETTER TO DARE MIGHTY THINGS, TO WIN GLORIOUS TRIUMPHS EVEN THOUGH CHECKERED BY FAILURE, THAN TO RANK WITH THOSE POOR SPIRITS WHO NEITHER ENJOY MUCH NOR SUFFER MUCH BECAUSE THEY LIVE IN THE GREY TWILIGHT THAT KNOWS NOT VICTORY OR DEFEAT."
>
> **PRESIDENT THEODORE ROOSEVELT**

STRATEGY

OK. We've looked at leadership from a few different perspectives and how important it is to get out of your own way; how to dig deep and get your foundation in place to change your life; and start wearing YOUR RED, whatever that means to you.

Now let's get to work on your plan—your strategy.

For those of you who have ever worked in a strategic planning process, creating a strategy and plan for your own self-development is not that different, except that we are focusing on YOU, not a business. To start building the structure of where you are going and who you are going to become, we need to start with one room at a time. Just like building a house, you have to start with a dream, then the design and then actual construction, one beam, one nail, one pour of concrete at a time. The entire process needs to be carefully planned out, one step at a time, each one building on the next.

So starting with your dream—your vision—is critical to getting to the end results. So, let's begin with getting your North Star firmly in place, so we can begin to breakdown the building process into manageable pieces.

YOUR TRUE NORTH (VISION, VALUES, MISSION)

We talked about vision in the beginning of the book and I asked the questions, "When was the last time you went on vacation? Or are you in the midst of planning one in the future?" Then, we walked through all the things we think about and do to plan that vacation and then make it happen. Think back to what that brought to mind or what you actually wrote down when you read that chapter and paint the picture in greater detail.

Now, think the same way about your life and career. Do you know where you are going? What you will pack? How you will get there and what you will do? I cannot stress how important it is to know where True North is for you and what that looks like! This picture, direction, will manifest itself in the deepest parts of your mind and will help you to see opportunities and potential as they enter your life so that you can move forward toward your vision.

To get you started, here is a quick exercise that can be very revealing. You can use this for anything you desire, need or want in your life. I have used and continue to use this during those times when I know exactly the result I want to create, but am uncertain how to get there.

Write down the result that you want to achieve. This can be anything that is important to you: a relationship (the man list or woman list), a car, a new client, a promotion, a house, a career, a trip, you get the idea. Once you have the one thing you want to accomplish, do this:

- Write your ONE THING at the top of a piece of paper.
- Draw a vertical line down the center of a piece of paper.
- On the left side, write down all the things you absolutely MUST have in this one thing.

- On the right side of the paper, write down all the things you WANT to have in this one thing.
- Focus on the MUST haves. As you work toward your ONE THING, measure every opportunity, person, situation or decision against your must haves, does it fit—does it meet your must-haves? If it does, continue—if it does not, move on.

Wash, rinse, repeat for every ONE THING on your list!

This simple process helps us make decisions based on our most deeply held beliefs and values and serves as a guide to following your True North and fulfilling your vision.

By the way, there is No app for that. None needed.

THE FIVE POINTED STAR – ORGANIZING THE STRATEGY

I first learned about the five-pointed star many years ago, when I was going through my initial facilitator and coach training and certification processes with Resource Associates Corporation. Since then, I have used it time and time and again as an organizational visual for clients—both on the personal and professional sides of life.

It is a graphic illustration of what successful people and companies do and how they think to create success and achieve goals. Each point of the star cannot exist without the other and each supports and integrates with other to achieve predetermined goals and objectives.

Every single detail and part of what you want to achieve falls into one of the points on the star. And when you align your thinking, behavior and actions in this way—you create a force of alignment that drives greater productivity, focus and goal achievement.

Think about this in terms of both your personal and professional life. Here is how it works:
- The top of the star is your Vision, Values & Purpose
- The upper-right point is your Structure
- The lower-right point is your Process
- The upper-left point is People
- And the lower-left is recognition and collaboration

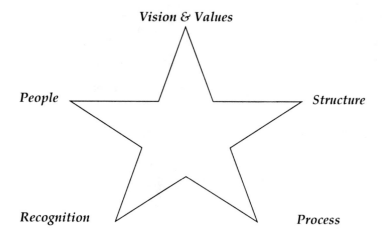

Each of the points on the star are connected to, aligned with, and support the Vision and Values. This is critical to staying on track and avoiding vision creep.

Now think about what details of your vision, goals and results fit into each point on the star—and write them down.

For example:

Vision & Values—let's say your vision is to circumvent the globe in a hot air balloon. Why is this important to you? Think about your values—perhaps you are driven to challenge

Chapter 7 - Leadership & Strategy

your strength and resolve with daring and risky adventure, or you want to prove to the world that one woman (or man) can accomplish anything with determination and grit, that belief, courage and beating the odds are at the core of who you are. OK, great, this is your vision and these are your values.

Structure—Now, what is the structure you will build around achieving this vision (all driven by your values)? You will need a map, guidance systems, equipment, the balloon, gear, food, the right clothes, etc. In other words, you need to build a plan for the trip—a structure to support everything you will need and do along the journey.

Process—Then, what are the processes you will have in place that support the structure and drive the vision (fueled by values)? How will you keep the balloon aloft? How will you feed, clothe and protect yourself against the elements? How will you maintain and repair the equipment? How will you find your way—navigate the trip?

People—will you need others to assist in any way? How? When? In what way? Why would they help you?

Reward and Collaboration—how will you reward and recognize the contribution of others along your journey and when it is completed? How will you be sure everyone is on the same page and collaborating to help you fulfill your vision? Are they in alignment with your values? Your structure? Your Process?

What does success look like?

These are all questions we need to ask ourselves when we begin any kind of journey—whether it be starting a new company, career, personal pursuit, or taking our life to the next level of success and happiness.

What does your five-pointed star look like?

BIG HAIRY AUDACIOUS GOALS – BHAGS & BDAGS

Once you determine what your five-pointed star looks like, then the real planning begins. Engage your left brain and start designing your future, your way.

Become the captain of your own ship. Put planning around your goals and dreams and take 100% responsibility for your life—every single bit. Uncover the "never wear red" thoughts and inhibitors rolling around in your head and CREATE <u>your life</u>. Step up and out. Have your vision and values firmly planted in your heart and mind and have a plan to create the life and legacy you desire.

The steps in your plan:
- Vision & Values
  - BHAGs & BDAGs
- Mission & Critical Goal Categories
- Why Smart Goals
- Action Steps
- Results
- Wash, Rinse, Repeat

Now that you have your vision and values **written down,** let's talk about BHAGs and BDAGs.

BHAGs – Big Hairy Audacious Goals aka DREAMS!

When was the last time you took time to simply DREAM? And I don't mean the modified, adult, serious dreams—I mean the dreams we used to dream as kids? Remember the opening to this book? I believed I could I fly. And indeed, I still do, but there was a time, a very long time, when I stopped believing I could fly—I stopped dreaming. Have you?

What are your dreams? Whether you ever believe they can come true or not—start writing them down in a dream inventory. Seriously. Challenge yourself to write 25 a week and see where that takes you! Ask your friends, family and co-workers what their dreams are and start the conversation! We need to dream more to become more. And no dream is off limits—the sky is the limit!!!

Write them down. These become your big hairy audacious goals. It's just plain fun to do this—makes me smile every time I do. And a funny thing happens along the way. You write down a bunch of your dreams and then like most everyone else, they get put aside for a while. Then, one day, you pick them up again and start reading through them and oh my, you discover that you have actually made some of them come true!

Magic?

You tell me.

BDAGs – Bold Daring Audacious Gals!

One of the greatest ways to test and push your BHAGs is to have BDAGs backing you up. These are your Bold Daring Audacious Gals (or Guys). A group of stakeholders, trusted friends and advisors that challenge, support, question and push you to be your very best and stay true to you, and live your dreams.

I am lucky to have a small, but mighty group of BDAGs in my

life. Each of them is a trusted, respected and admired friend and colleague and each has been, and continues to be, invaluable in helping me to realize my dreams and move closer to my vision.

BDAGs help each other to make game changing decisions, face uncertainty, deal with trauma, go up against the odds, face fears and take 100% responsibility in our businesses and in our lives. It's not always easy, but certainly a game changer. Find yourself your BDAGs.

MISSION & CRITICAL GOAL CATEGORIES

Once you have started to identify your BHAGs, it's time to prioritize the ones that are most immediate and crucial to meeting your current goals and achieving the results you want to get in a specific period of time.

First, write out a statement that clearly outlines what you will accomplish (as aligned to your vision and values) in the next six to eighteen months. Be specific. This is your MISSION, should you choose to accept it. Mission statements are changed as you move toward your vision. They break down the Vision into smaller, manageable chunks so you can plan out the steps to achieve your goals in a timely and accountable way.

Once you have your Mission statement and you know what you will accomplish in the next specified period of time, break out the categories—or buckets as I like to call them—of things you need to work on. Depending upon what your overarching vision is, one bucket may be research, or marketing, or operations, or personnel, or resources needed, or knowledge needed, or finances, etc. Create three to six buckets of critical areas that are part of this particular mission statement. These are your Critical Goal Categories (CGCs).

These categories are where you will focus your energy and time for the duration of this particular mission statement. Now, prioritize the buckets. Each bucket can only be one number. You cannot have two buckets as priority #1 – it just doesn't work that way! You may need to move between the buckets as you go along, but each must still have its own priority number.

Now, line up the CGCs in a table:

CGC #1	CGC#2	CGC#3

WHYSMART Goals

Now that you have your critical goal categories established, each of those categories needs to be narrowed down into WHY SMART goals.

Most of us know the acronym for SMART when it comes to goal setting; specific, measurable, attainable, realistic and time bound. But add the WHY to the start of this acronym and we have narrowed the focus of goal setting even further. Now the goals are WRITTEN; HARMONIOUS; and YOURS.

A good friend of mine who just happens to be a prolific and well-known writer once told me, "Rox, nothing is real until it is written". I have never forgotten that! If I asked you if you had goals, you would most likely respond that you do. Most people would. But if I asked if I could see your 'goal list' or journal or spreadsheet, would you have anything to show me? Most people would not.

A goal is not a goal unless it is written. It is only an idea, a thought, a dream, a desire or a want until it is written. How many times have you had a great idea or goal pop into your head that you absolutely HAD to accomplish, only to have it disappear as soon as the next phone call, instant message, text or interruption happened. Right. Write it down!

And write it down in the category (CGC) in which in belongs. Do that with all of your goals. Your WHYSMART goals are the things you need to do to accomplish what you need to accomplish to fulfill the critical goal category. Once the CGC has been completed, wash-rinse-repeat! Create a new mission for the next 6 to 12 months and create new CGCs to accomplish the new mission. Guess what? You are now making progress!

CGC #1	CGC#2	CGC#3
WSG #1	WSG #1	WSG #1
WSG #2	WSG #2	WSG #2
WSG #3	WSG #3	WSG #3

Be sure that as you approach your WHYSMART goals under each CGC that they are prioritized in order of importance so that you are only concentrating on what must be done first in order to move to the next goal. Keep it simple and attainable.

Imagine, what would your life be like if you were able to focus your attention on your three top priorities for one week? What if you were able to concentrate, focus and actually complete those activities, in spite of the usual distractions?

"In the final analysis, the quality of our life depends on our ability to consciously choose who and what we give our thoughts, interests moments and emotions to."—Author Sam Horn, in Concentrate: Get Focused and Pay Attention—When Life Is Filled With Pressures, Distractions, and Multiple Priorities (2000).

Concentration is becoming a lost art—for me, too! It is such an important part of our lives, yet we are losing sight of it. Life is all about what we pay attention to. If we are paying all of our attention on the trivial, meaningless things—our lives will reflect exactly that—the trivial and meaningless. If we put our attention and focus on meaningful, positive things, again, our lives will reflect that and we'll have a meaningful, positive life. This is profoundly simple, and one of life's great truths.

"Our experience is what we attend to." —William James

If we chronically multi-task and engage in scattered thoughts and noise all of the time, we will have scattered, noisy and chaotic lives. The fast-paced world we live in is very distracting. We are constantly bombarded by information, e-mail, phone calls and news.

Multi-tasking is a myth. Human beings cannot do more than one thing at a time, if they want to do one thing well.

Learning or re-learning the art of focus and concentration helps us focus on and in the moment, instead of frantically rushing from moment to moment. The Pareto Principle says that 80 percent of our results comes from only 20 percent of our efforts. That means that only about 20 percent of our activities actually provide the results we are looking for.

So what would your life look like—how would it be different—

if you devoted more time and energy to the crucial 20 percent of your activities? Might you accomplish more, have better relationships, and more life satisfaction? Why not give it a try for a day? A week? A month? It might turn into a great lifetime habit!

 **GO FOR GOLD**

- Your North Star is your guide. Your vision of the future. Once you have your vision, then you need to start planning the journey to get there—one step at a time. Start with your one thing that you want to accomplish in the immediate future. Make your list of must-dos and should-dos and get started. Once the first one is completed, move on to the next. Wash, rinse, repeat.
- 5-Pointed Star—draw it and fill it in—Vision; Structure; Process; People; Recognition. All five connect and support each other. This is your roadmap.
- Big harry audacious goals are dreams that become reality. What are yours? Start a Dream Inventory. Write 25 a week each week for a month, then you can go to about 5 a week.
- Form you group of BDAGS. The trusted advisors who push you to do your best and hold you accountable.
- Write your mission; critical goal categories and then fill in your WHY SMART goals. Voila! You have just completed a strategic plan!

CHAPTER 8

MEETING OLD FRIENDS FOR THE FIRST TIME

> TRUST IS THE GLUE OF LIFE.
>
> IT'S THE MOST ESSENTIAL INGREDIENT IN EFFECTIVE COMMUNICATION.
>
> IT'S THE FOUNDATIONAL PRINCIPLE THAT HOLDS ALL RELATIONSHIPS.
>
> **STEPHEN COVEY**

JAMES TAYLOR WROTE and Carol King sang *"You've Got a Friend."* What a wonderful thing it is to know we have a friend or friends out there who have our back. Who will be there when we need them. Who believe in us, no matter what.

What would it be like if we approached strangers with the idea that they were one of these friends we were simply meeting for the first time? How would that change things?

You have probably had times in your life when you have felt out of place, insecure and unsure of yourself. I've never met anyone who has not experienced this at least a few times in their life. Just think of the dreaded networking event. From what I've heard and experienced, most people dread these things, but we do it anyway—usually in the attempt to meet new people and

Chapter 8 - Meeting Old Friends for The First Time

grow our contacts and businesses. Not to mention the influence of that old adage from our adolescence running through our minds—"Don't talk to strangers."

When I first started out on my own, I was no different. After all, who was I to think I could be a success on my own? But I was determined and knew I HAD to get myself out there and start growing my network and my tribe, as I call it. But I very quickly became tired of dreading these things and as a result, not being very productive.

And then it occurred to me that I was approaching this in all the wrong ways. Remember when we talked about attitude and keeping an open mind in Chapter 6? Well, that is exactly what I needed to do—change my attitude! So, as I reflected on all the wonderful relationships I had built so far in my life, I realized every single person I now called friend was a stranger at first. And now they were old and dear friends.

That's when it hit me—what if, instead of going out to meet strangers and see if we could become friends and colleagues, I got up every morning knowing I was going to meet old friends for the first time? BAM! Game changer! Now, the reality is the next old friend you meet for the first time may only be a friend for 5 minutes—maybe 10 or 15—or maybe a lifetime or somewhere in between. But that is not the point. The point is ATTITUDE. When you approach other human beings with an attitude of openness, authenticity, genuine curiosity and yes, friendship those other human beings respond in kind and you have each just met an old friend.

Imagine how this will change the conversation, engage another person and actually create an enjoyable, and dare I say, fun experience. Talking with a friend is always so much more rewarding than talking to a stranger—give it try. It may take a bit of practice, but do it. You could very possibly start looking forward to those networking events. OK—maybe that's a push, but you never know!

Bottom line is this:

No matter where you are in your life and career right now as you read these words, the road can get rough. The more support we have—both internally and externally—the easier it is to navigate the rough spots. So why wouldn't we do everything we can every day to strengthen our support systems? And part of that is an attitude of meeting old friends for the first time every day.

So, when you want to give-up, quit, not attend that event or not follow-up on that promise or commitment because you are just not feeling it, pause and take stock of where you are and how you got here. Chances are there are other people involved. People who have helped, hindered, encouraged and challenged— and all who have helped you learn a lesson about who you are and what you are made of. Find more people to meet, know and learn about and you will increase your learning and growing curve exponentially.

All of this takes what is now called "Emotional Intelligence." I used to call this common sense, intuition, grace, empathy and compassion, but I love EI. It is exactly what each of us needs to develop and nurture in ourselves and our relationships throughout our lives. It starts with our own inner Champion. Here is where our best self, resides.

How emotionally intelligent are you? How can you up the bar in this area of your growth and development? And if you can how will that help you? We need to understand what motivates us and how our relationships play into our success, or fear and failure. We all need a support system of some kind to remind us of how special and unique we are when that is the last thing we believe in any given moment. This support can come from old friends, colleagues or family or, an old friend you have just met for the first time.

All of this is a matter of choice—our choice—remember, we are 100% responsible for where we are right now. Let's talk about EI.

EMOTIONAL INTELLIGENCE

From a quick scan on google, here is a basic definition of EI (or EQ, as some call it)

e·mo·tion·al in·tel·li·gence (also referred to as Emotional Quotient – EQ)

noun

The capacity to be aware of, control, and express one's emotions, and to handle interpersonal relationships judiciously and empathetically.

According to TalentSmart®, a premier, worldwide provider of emotional intelligence (EQ) learning and training:

"Emotional intelligence is the 'something' in each of us that is a bit intangible. It affects how we manage behavior, navigate social complexities, and make personal decisions that achieve positive results. Emotional intelligence is made up of four core skills that pair up under two primary competencies: personal competence and social competence."

According to TalentSmart® statistics:

Emotional Intelligence

(EQ) Stats

Learn More About EQ

So, what exactly does this mean? What is it? How do we get it or get more of it?

There is a great article on the web at <u>http://www.talentsmart.com/about/emotional-intelligence.php</u> that will take you through an excellent explanation of emotional intelligence. In the meantime, here is an overview of the key points:

Emotional intelligence was first introduced in 1995. It was the first time a school of thought came into being that talked about something other than the Intelligence Quotient (IQ) as being the key to success.

It upended a lot of thinking and presumptions on the part of many an esteemed scholar, but none the less, began to take root as not only incredibly powerful, but a very real, yet intangible, measurement of success.

Here is a bit of the history of the development of EI from <u>http://www.emotionalintelligencecourse.com/eq-history</u>:

"Peter Salovey and John D. Mayer coined the term 'Emotional Intelligence' in 1990 describing it as *"a form of social intelligence that involves the ability to monitor one's own and others' feelings and emotions, to discriminate among them, and to use this information to guide one's thinking and action."*

"In the 1990's Daniel Goleman became aware of Salovey and Mayer's work, and this eventually led to his book, <u>Emotional Intelligence</u>. Goleman was a science writer for the New York Times, specialising in brain and behaviour research. He trained as a psychologist at Harvard where he worked with David McClelland, among others. McClelland was among a growing group of researchers who were becoming concerned with how little traditional tests of cognitive intelligence told us about what it takes to be successful in life."

Goleman argued that it was not cognitive intelligence that guaranteed business success but emotional intelligence. He described emotionally intelligent people as those with four characteristics:

1. They were good at understanding their own emotions (self-awareness)
2. They were good at managing their emotions (self-management)
3. They were empathetic to the emotional drives of other people (social awareness)
4. They were good at handling other people's emotions (social skills)

And so, EI (EQ) was introduced to the masses. Funny, I thought this was something that everyone knew when I first heard the term. I was surprised this was a new school of thought.

Chapter 8 - Meeting Old Friends for The First Time

Doesn't it just make sense that human beings are more successful and happy when they have a good balance of their left and right brains? It certainly did to me, but that is in no way disrespecting Salovey, Mayer, Goleman, Travis Bradberry, Jean Greaves and others who have done and continue to do extraordinary research, work and development in this area. They have opened up a whole new perspective and applicable set of learnable skills to increase the quality of our lives in all aspects and create more success and happiness for ourselves and others.

Here are the main areas of focus in developing our Emotional Intelligence:

Personal Competencies	Social Competencies

And each one of these two categories has core skills associated with it:

Personal Competencies	Social Competencies
• Self-awareness	• Social-awareness
• Self-management	• Relationship-management
• Motivation	

And each core skill has specific areas of thought and behavior:

Personal Competencies	Social Competencies
• Self-awareness	• Social-awareness
• Emotional	• Understanding others
• Self-assessment	• Service orientation
• Self-confidence	• Leveraging diversity
• Self-management	• Political awareness
• Self-control	• Relationship-management
• Trustworthiness	• Developing others
• Conscientiousness	• Influence
• Adaptability	• Communication
• Innovation	• Conflict management
• Motivation	• Leadership
• Achievement drive	• Change catalyst
• Commitment	• Building bonds
• Initiative	• Collaboration and cooperation
• Optimism	• Teamwork

And the good news is this can all be developed and learned. These are all learned skills—just like leadership! There is an abundance of research and information online, including books, articles and white papers and I encourage you to take a look.

Becoming a leader, having an awareness of what your "Never Wear Red" conditioning is and overcoming it, becoming and being the best version of yourself, all of these things require life-long learning and a desire to understand oneself and others in a way and with insight you have not had before.

Understanding and developing our own Emotional Intelligence is an important, no wait, critical, element to who we become and the quality of the relationships we form. We certainly do need more leaders—genuine, authentic leaders in our world who are willing to step up with awareness and knowledge of how emotions play in our relationships and in our world and help to make it better rather than more divisive, angry and hostile.

OK—I will stop there before I go off on a rant and get back to our love story, our love of the liberation of self—to be, do and become our own best champion!

Final thought - Look for old friends to meet wherever you go. You will be surprised by who shows up.

> "I REALLY THINK THAT THERE WAS A GREAT ADVANTAGE IN MANY WAYS TO BEING A WOMAN. I THINK WE ARE A LOT BETTER AT PERSONAL RELATIONSHIPS, AND THEN HAVE THE CAPABILITY OBVIOUSLY OF TELLING IT LIKE IT IS WHEN IT'S NECESSARY."
>
> **MADELEINE ALBRIGHT**

MOTIVATION

None of this self-awareness and development, overcoming challenges and obstacles, seeing our vision of success and happiness, setting and accomplishing goals, wearing whatever our personal red may be—would be possible without the internal motivation to make it happen.

So where does this kind of sustainable motivation come from? How do we get it and keep it?

Sometimes the motivation comes from what we do NOT want and what we want to change or eliminate in our lives. Remember the story about how I decided to end my corporate career and start my own firm? The motivation behind that decision was to get away from something that had become a negative in my life and no longer had a positive impact on my life or the person I wanted to be and to become.

My guess is that you too have some things (or people) in your life that are not giving you the opportunity to be and to become your best self. Think about where you are right now—work, relationships, happiness, success—are you where you want to be? If so, fantastic! Well done. If not, what is in your way? What is your motivation to make the changes necessary to start moving your life, career, emotional, intellectual and spiritual well-being, family, social and business relationships in a better and more fulfilling direction?

On the other hand, sometimes the motivation comes from what we DO want to bring into our lives and into our own growth as a person. Make your 'list' of must haves (the non-negotiables) and want-to-haves and start making a plan to manifest these into your life.

Whether it is to STOP doing or participating (going away from), or, to START doing or participating (going towards) in relationships, work, et al—what will it take to awaken your desire and internal motivation to DO SOMETHING and to take 100% responsibility of YOU?

6 COMPONENTS OF HIDDEN MOTIVATION

Now let's put this whole topic of motivation into practical terms in regard to getting your plan together working with others to make it happen. It makes no difference what the setting is in which you are working with other people, the principles here are the same.

Ed Muzio, President and CEO of Group Harmonics, explains what drives people to perform and why understanding motivation – in yourself and others – can be incredibly impactful in creating clearer communication and trust between people. Here is the link to his video on YouTube.

https://www.youtube.com/watch?v=GZ_VuA_noYk

So, of the six hidden factors of motivation – what is your strongest motivator – what drives your thoughts and behavior?

1. Truth – learning the truth and finding the right answers.
2. Results – getting the ROI and driving everything to the bottom-line.
3. Power – it needs to be all about you, your role, your authority.
4. Assistance – it is all about helping others.
5. Form – your subjective experience (harmony, form, beauty, people).
6. Structure – repeatable processes, same results, same rules.

After you view the video—translate this into an internal dialogue with yourself and ask what your primary motivator is—and then apply that to what you want to make happen in both your professional and personal life. For me, it is all about Assistance and Form. And these are both (in different words) at the heart of what I do, everyday.

What are yours?

Once you know—let others know! This is as much about understanding what motivates others as it is about what motivates you, and we need to let others know. Advertise your motivators! This is another way of knowing and living your WHY.

Wear YOUR Red.

MYTHS

A few words on the danger of myths.

A myth is a widely held, but false belief or idea. How many of these get in imbedded in our brains and become one those self-limiting beliefs that prevent us from becoming the best we can be and leave us stuck in mediocrity?

My guess is a lot.

Repetition is the way we humans learn. Remember your multiplication tables? Flash cards? When we hear the same thing over and over again, it becomes imbedded in our brains—whether it is true or not—and we believe it. Think of advertising. The advertising world is based on this to a large degree—that's why we see the same ads over again—so we remember the truth we are being told and then take action (buy the product) to have that truth in our lives.

It makes sense that if this kind of repetition works with both facts (math and spelling) and with myths (as with some advertising), then it would stand to reason that if you are told certain things about yourself often enough (whether true or false) you begin to believe it and know it is true without question. It becomes a habit of thought.

I mentioned this earlier in the chapter about attitude and what it really is and is not. It is a thought that gets imbedded in your subconscious mind, and becomes REAL to you. The subconscious mind tells your conscious mind this thought—and tells it as if it is true. Your subconscious mind does not know the difference between a truth and non-truth—so you KNOW it is true and do not question it. Your behavior and actions then follow your thoughts and you get the result of your actions.

For example, let's say you have been told since you were a small child that you could not sing. You have a terrible voice and no one wants to hear you screech.

At first, you don't really believe this, so you continue to sing songs you hear on the radio, YouTube, iTunes, etc. You forget that you cannot sing. But then someone hears you singing and tells you again to STOP! You cannot sing! People are laughing and poking fun at you every time you open your mouth.

As you grow older, you are quiet when everyone else is singing in church or caroling during the holidays. When you are asked to join a choir, or join in around the piano and sing, you smile and respond, "Oh no, I can't sing. I'll just listen."

How much are you missing out on because you believe you cannot sing? What else are you not doing, trying, learning, risking because you were told:

You are not smart enough...

You are not pretty or handsome enough...

You are a wallflower...

You are not outgoing enough...

And I know there are hundreds more examples. The point is, these myths will stop you in your tracks every time if you let them. Don't let them. Do not take what anyone says as YOUR truth, explore it first and really understand WHO you are and what your real strengths and challenges are and then follow your plan to achieve and do what you set out do.

Bust the myths. Igniting your plan depends on it.

 **GO FOR GOLD**

- Change your attitude about getting yourself out there. Relationships are the key to building a business, a career, a life of meaning and value. Change your mindset from don't talk to strangers and the dread of networking and meeting new people to a mind-set of looking forward to meeting old friends for the first time—every day. It changes the conversation and it changes the ordinary to the extraordinary. Who knows? It may even change your life.

- Emotional Intelligence is equally, if not more, important than IQ. What is your level of EI? These kinds of assessments allow us to see ourselves in a different way. And although they are not the be all and end all of who we are, they certainly give us insight to our strengths and areas of improvement. Take some assessments and use the results to help guide your path to extraordinary leadership.

- Six Things—what are your motivators? Ed Muzio shows us six that are particularly important in working with others. Write down yours and then share this information with whom you work and play. It's also great conversation starter for those times when you are meeting old friends for the first time!

- Watch out for myths that have morphed into truths and become negative habits of thought in your head. When one of those pops up, train your brain to be aware of it and counteract it with a reverse thought. Write these down so you can reference them every time they occur. Myths like to derail you—you are smarter than the myth!

CHAPTER 9

DON'T LOOK BACK – YOU ARE NOT GOING THAT WAY.

> DESIRE IS THE KEY TO MOTIVATION, BUT IT'S DETERMINATION AND COMMITMENT TO AN UNRELENTING PURSUIT OF YOUR GOAL - A COMMITMENT TO EXCELLENCE - THAT WILL ENABLE YOU TO ATTAIN THE SUCCESS YOU SEEK.
>
> **MARIO ANDRETTI**

THE MYTHS THAT WE just talked about can and will sideline the best intentions to IGNITE your plan of accomplishment and success. This negative conditioning is part of growing up. We just don't realize it when it's happening, nor do we understand the long-term effects on our development as leaders. We are all products of our past. This chapter talks about past conditioning, how to recognize it and break it down into manageable chunks so we can diffuse it and change our behavior. Then, tracking the results and keeping it all in balance is key to long term success and implementing solutions.

It's imperative to keep in mind, that although outside influences have a big impact on our own self-image, so do self-talk and attitudes. Self-limiting thoughts and self-destructive behaviors can be the most debilitating of all. I use the following story/legend often when I am working with groups or individuals on developing self-awareness and positive attitudes.

A Cherokee Legend - Two Wolves

One evening an old Cherokee told his grandson about a battle that goes on inside people. He said, "My son, the battle is between two 'wolves' inside us all.

One is Evil. It is anger, envy, jealousy, sorrow, regret, greed, arrogance, self-pity, guilt, resentment, inferiority, lies, false pride, superiority, and ego.

The other is Good. It is joy, peace, love, hope, serenity, humility, kindness, benevolence, empathy, generosity, truth, compassion and faith."

The grandson thought about it for a minute and then asked his grandfather:

"Which wolf wins?"

The old Cherokee simply replied, "The one you feed."

What side of yourself are you feeding? The one that believes all the negative conditioning and myths that you have been told and that you tell yourself over and over again? Or the one deep inside your heart that you know is the real and true you? This is the one made of gold. It takes strength and determination to dig it out.

Ghosts

Mixed in with the negative conditioning we face as we grow up, are the ghosts from the past that like to show up—always at the worst of times—and haunt us about the woulda, shoulda, coulda's.

These spectors have really loud voices and can be a serious distraction to our own well-being, growth, development and progress in our leadership journey.

Even when we are singularly focused on determining our future with the best of intention and focus, a ghost will jump into our brain and start derailing our thoughts, goals, behavior and actions. It's probably safe to say that for most people, this happens more than we would like—and often times we are not even aware it is happening.

So why does this happen? Why do our brains do this? Well, the brain is complicated machine.

Shawn Achor is the author of the international best seller, *"The Happiness Advantage"* and another book entitled, *"Before Happiness: the 5 Hidden Keys to Achieving Success, Spreading Happiness and Sustaining Positive Change"*.

In the *"Before Happiness"* book, Shawn talks about the 5 hidden keys, the third of which is canceling internal noise.

Chapter 9 - Don't Look Back – You Are Not Going That Way.

Shawn talks about ways to cancel the internal noise, not by just blocking it, but replacing it with positive thoughts and energy. This directly relates to our previous discussion of affirmations. You can change the way you think! The important thing to know and remember is that YOU control your thoughts - your thoughts DO NOT control you - unless you allow them to control you.

Shawn writes, *"Pessimism, one of the most common and pervasive forms of internal noise, is a defense mechanism your brain puts up to try to minimize the impact of negative events you experience in life."*

I encourage you to take a look at Shawn's website for more information and insights on this topic! He is an expert in this area http://goodthinkinc.com/speaking/shawn-achor/

When we consider all of this as we work toward ghost busting, getting out of our own way, and designing a strategy to ignite our vision, we need to be careful HOW we are thinking and planning the future.

Consider this:

- If we look to the past to guide our present, we will simply recreate the past.
- If we look at the present to guide our future, we will recreate the past and the present.
- If we forecast into the future to guide our future, we will create a forecast.
- If, however, we <u>decide</u> what our future will be—<u>we will create it.</u>

Decide. Now. What do you want your future to be? This is an incredibly important part of building your plan and executing on your strategy. This is where you are going. Exciting! And it requires discipline, focus, knowing what obstacles may cross your path (even if it is YOU) and thinking ahead to solutions to overcome the obstacles.

Discipline

We can think about this word in a multitude of ways:

- As a noun: **discipline**—that speaks to the practice of training people to obey rules or a code of behavior, using punishment to correct disobedience.
- As a plural noun: **disciplines**—as a system of rules of conduct; a branch of knowledge, typically one studied in higher education.
- As a verb: **discipline:** train (someone) to obey rules or a code of behavior, using punishment to correct disobedience; train oneself to do something in a controlled and habitual way.

It's this last one—training ourselves to do something in a controlled and habitual way—that we need to remember to keep us focused on the present and future, not on the past.

I've had a little sign hanging on the inside of a cupboard door that I open every day. It says, "never let yesterday use up today." What a great reminder to discipline our brains, our thinking, every day to be in the PRESENT and to look with anticipation and excitement to the future!

Focus

You cannot continue to look behind you while moving forward without tripping! The past is done. It is over. Don't succumb to the evil wolf or the ghosts that speak to you about bad decisions, regrets, failures, mistakes, loss, betrayal and all the bad things that have happened or poor choices that you have made. Figure out your lessons, if you haven't already done so, apply the lessons to your life as you go along, and forgive yourself. And forgive others. There. You just grew a little bit. That weight on your shoulders should feel a bit lighter.

Obstacles & Solutions

Look forward and do so with another simple, yet very effective formula.

1. Establish your objective—clearly, specifically, precisely.
2. What are the obstacles that are, or could, get in your way? (hint—You; Wolf; Ghost?)
3. What are the rewards for accomplishing this objective? (these should be an extreme feel good)
4. What are the consequences if do not? (these should be an extreme NOOOOOOOOOOOO!)
5. What are the solutions to the obstacles? (hint—go back and reread all previous chapters in this book—the solutions are there)
6. What action steps do you need to take and when—to achieve your objective.

That's it. That is the discipline that's needed to move forward into each moment; develop your internal leadership; positively impact your success and happiness; and maybe, just maybe—make a difference in someone else's life and dare I say it—the world?

 **GO FOR GOLD**

- Be aware of the ghosts that pop up and try to distract you from your purpose and goals. Invite them in for tea and they will disappear! Don't avoid them, embrace them, and they will run scared. They are mist—they are fog—trying to muddy the waters. Look 'em in the eye and move on. They will not hang around.
- It takes dedication, determination and discipline to be a leader of self and others. What are the things you need to do every day to maintain your discipline to accomplish what you have set out to do? Write them down and follow them every day.
- Take a moment to think about the obstacles that are, or could be, in your way of accomplishing your goals and vision. What are they (and remember, the biggest one may be the one you see in the mirror). Write them down and then write down two or three solutions for each of them and the action steps needed to overcome the obstacle.

PART III

IMPACT

"Action is the foundational key to all success."

Pablo Picasso

Two of the three 'i's are now in the works for you. You have your inspiration and you are working on igniting.

Now its time for the third 'i'—impact.

How many times do we have a great idea, put a plan together—see ourselves succeeding in bringing the idea to light—only to never actually DO anything with it? More often than we care to admit would be my guess.

A few years ago, I decided it was MY year to get focused on my body and get really toned, strong and lean. I bought a treadmill, weights, really cool workout clothes and shoes, fitness DVD's for my workouts, wrote a vision statement of the Wonder Woman I was going to become, wrote a strategic plan and action steps and was super excited to get started!

Then life happened.

A month later, I looked at all my cool gear and realized that I actually had to use it—take action—to make my vision a reality. Just because I bought a treadmill did not mean that I would become more fit. If we want to make a change, achieve a goal, fulfill our potential—we must take action.

An idea, a vision, a plan, a desire, a passion, a goal are only words and pictures in our head and on paper when we choose to record them. None of these things become anything other than that unless we actually DO something.

And action requires motivation. Remember the stories in the beginning of this section about the elephants and frogs and how they had been conditioned to believing in limitations that did not exist? It is the same with us. We need to see beyond our limitations (self-imposed and otherwise) to find the motivation to take action on the things we want to accomplish in our lives. Remember that motivation comes from two sources—external or internal. The external motivators are generated by something or someone outside of ourselves. In business, a raise, promotion, a move to the corner office—are all examples of positive external motivators to accomplish something and to achieve a specific goal, it's the reward. The opposite is also true—if you do not achieve the goal or accomplish what is expected of you, you are demoted, you do not receive the bonus, you are fired—all external negative motivators.

The most powerful motivation, however, is internal. It is your own desire to achieve a desired outcome and is 100% in your control. Much more appealing than dangling carrot in someone's else's control—don't you think?

The first two i's—inspire and ignite—are essential to getting to this third and final i. In my experience with clients, in my own life, and in reading research about the complexities of the human brain, we really can accomplish anything we put our minds to. Every human brain has the same capacity for learning as every other human brain (unless damaged in some way). Here is a great 9 minute video that explains much about how are brains work:

https://www.youtube.com/watch?v=Y4O_Wkv66b0

"This video was published on Nov 28, 2012. It was produced by http://www.useyourbrainforsuccess.com.au. Enter the fascinating realm of how your brain works in this short, simple and easy to understand video. Be amazed at how much unrealised potential you have. The reality is that no one is any smarter and clever than anyone else, the difference lies in understanding how to unlock your brain's power and potential. Life can be a level playing field when you learn to tap into your brain's amazing potential. For more information and resources go to http://www.useyourbrainforsuccess.com"

So with this in mind, let's start on the steps to unlock your brain so you can do your best work and accomplish the greatest of tasks. It's time to tap into your internal motivation and combine your passion, vision, goals, the plan and start creating your future!

 ACTION! IMPACT!

CHAPTER 10

DO OR DO NOT. THERE IS NO TRY.
YODA

EXECUTE. A GREAT VISION, a great plan—mean nothing unless we execute and achieve results. We can try to execute, or, we can execute. The difference is failure or success!

Pull together all the pieces of your plan that you have created thus far, and put them into the following pages to create your master planning document that will guide you toward realizing your goals and eventually your vision. As you do so, don't forget to incorporate the people and resources you will need to execute on the plan. This is your web of the people who are influencers, confidantes and supporters of your quest—and the resources they and you need to accomplish the goals you set forward.

Before we go further, let's revisit the whole attitude thing one more time. It is so important to accomplishing anything.

Our attitudes help us to form not only our own self-leadership, but also the leadership of others. When attitudes of leadership culminate, they create cultures of leadership. These cultures of leadership build strong, sustainable companies and organizations because they **walk the talk, share vision, challenge process, empower others and genuinely engage others.** These are the five practices of exemplary leadership from The Leadership Challenge®. These five practices build stellar cultures of leadership.

And they need execution to make that happen. People doing what they say they will do.

How many leaders have you known that make big promises but rarely deliver on those promises? How does that make you feel about that person? Will you follow them willingly? Probably not. Leadership is about many things and a few of the most critical are accountability, action and getting results. People walking their talk.

Like leadership, execution is a learned skill. There is a specific set of behaviors and techniques that are taught and mastered in order to create a culture of execution. It's more than a tactic—it is a discipline and a system. It is built into a company's strategy, goals, and culture, with the leaders of the organization deeply engaged.

In a 10-year study of winning companies, professors William Joyce and Nitin Nohria found four primary management practices that directly correlate with superior corporate performance, as measured by total return to shareholders: execution, strategy, culture, and structure (What Really Works, 2003).

Oftentimes, however, these processes become silos.

- Robust dialogue to surface the realities of the business.
- Accountability for results discussed openly and agreed to by those responsible for getting things done.
- Rewards for the best performers.
- Follow-through to ensure that progress tracks to the plans.

Are you trying to step up and execute effectively on your strategy?

Or are you doing it? Are you taking action?

Why or why not?

DO OR DO NOT. THERE IS NO TRY.

YODA

EXECUTING ON THE PLAN

So, by now, you have a pretty good idea of some of the obstacles (all those Never Wear Red influences) that have been standing in your way of creating your life, in your way, and in your time. You have also devised solutions to those obstacles and are ready to begin defining the action steps—the execution—that needs to happen to start moving you closer to your vision. Be sure you have these written down, you need to be reminded of these things often so that you can continue to overpower them with positive thoughts and action.

Here is the structure of your plan and how to move into the action phase, to make the impact you envision completing your *i to the power of 3.*

1. *inspire* – **vision, values & principles**

    a. The Vision is the dream we have of the future. It empowers us through all we do and keeps us focused on what we will accomplish. The Vision rarely changes—it is our guidepost for creating what we envision.

    b. Inspiration is found through a process of self-discovery, values and principles. Record the results of any assessments you have done—your strengths, genius, brilliance, talents and areas of growth. Start thinking, dreaming and envisioning the life you want and the person you want to become.

2. **Ignite—mission & critical goal categories**

   a. The mission is a broad statement of the areas of focus and what we will accomplish in specific period of time— usually 6-18 months. It is our priority statement of what needs to be done and what steps need to be taken to move us closer to our vision.

   b. Critical Goal Categories are the buckets—those large categories of priorities that we need to focus on over the next 6-18 months to achieve our goals and objectives. (Each CGC has its own WHY SMART goals—each of which has specific action steps, timelines and someone assigned to take responsibility for achieving the goals, usually YOU).

   c. Ignite your new self-knowledge with alignment to your CGC's—and begin to get a better understanding of what both personal and professional success and leadership are and are not for you. This is where you craft and record your strategic life and professional plans and begin to focus on and articulate your most important critical goals and what it will take to achieve them.

3. **Impact—why smart goals, action steps, results**

   a. Begin work on fine-tuning your focus to clearly determine specific impact and outcomes of your goals and actions. Through the alignment of your strengths, values, skills and knowledge to your own and to your organizational vision and goals, you can then identify your short and long-term goals and create specific timelines and action plans for achievement and success.

b. WHY SMART goals are written for each of the CGC's. These goals are Written, Harmonious (with the Vision), Yours and Specific, Measurable, Attainable, Realistic and Timely.

c. Each WHY SMART goal has specific action steps that will be taken within a specific timeframe to achieve the goal. These action steps have a person or people responsible for its achievement.

d. Celebrate the wins! Keep track of all the accomplishments and make them a part of every team meeting. Reflect on what is working and why and what is not and why. If deadlines are missed, look at the obstacles in the way and solutions for those obstacles. Then set a new action plan and get it done! If something is not working, determine why—the rewards or consequences of letting it go or keeping at it, then decide and move forward!

THE I3 PROCESS

DO.

Begin your plan.

Write your Vision Statement

Go back and look at your values again. Your top five and THE ONE core value that fuels everything you do and all that you are about. As you write your vision statement, keep these values uppermost in your mind and design you vision with you values as the foundation.

Be sure you write your vision statement in the present tense as if it has already happened. This helps your brain manifest the vision in real time as you move toward the vision.

If you already have a vision statement, take it out and see if you can make it even more vivid and compelling.

VISION STATEMENT

Values/Purpose/Principles

_____

_____

_____

_____

_____

_____

WRITE YOUR MISSION STATEMENT

The mission statement will change from time to time. This is a statement of what you will do in the next 6 to 18 months to move closer to your vision. This is where you start to prioritize what needs to be done first, second and so forth to move you closer to your vision. Think about what you need to accomplish and what it will look like when you have done so. What are the most important objectives that must be achieved over the next 6-18 months? Write it down in a statement.

MISSION STATEMENT

Over the next 6-18 months, I will focus on driving the vision through the following key **objectives** (what do you want to achieve?)

_____
_____
_____
_____
_____
_____

These objectives will be achieved through my **actions** of (what are you going to DO to achieve the objectives?)

_____
_____
_____
_____
_____
_____

WRITE YOUR CGC'S

Critical Goal Categories are the buckets or general areas of focus under which the smaller goals and specific action steps will fall. For example, CGC's may be things like—research, education, finances, networking, IT. These categories are the three to six top areas of focus and goal accomplishment over the next six to twelve months.

Your CGC's must align to the accomplishment of the next steps in manifesting and actualizing your vision and mission. Write out your buckets. No less than three and no more than six to accomplish in the six to eighteen months. Once these are accomplished then you will do the exact same again—write a new mission statement and CGC's for the next 6-18 months.

CRITICAL GOAL CATEGORIES

1) _____

2) _____

3) _____

4) _____

5) _____

6) _____

Once you have your CGCs established, it's time to write down the specific goals that need to be achieved in each of the categories. Break each category down into bite-sized pieces so that you can prioritize and manage each one within a specific time frame. These are your WHY SMART Goals. They are written; harmonious (with the CGC, vision and mission); yours (not anyone else's); specific; measurable; realistic; and timely.

Here is an example:

Why Smart Goals

1. **CGC #1 <u>Research Learning Leadership</u>**
   WS Goals
   - Read the book "Learning Leadership" by Jim Kouzes & Barry Posner
   - Interview 20 people who are using the concepts and track their results
   - Create a spreadsheet of the results
   - Write a white paper on the findings and publish on LinkedIn

2. **CGC #2** _____
   WS Goals
   -
   -
   -
   -

3. **CGC #3** _____
   WS Goals
   -
   -
   -

4. **CGC #4** _____
   WS Goals
   -

-
-
-
-
-

Now, each of the WHY SMART goals has specific action steps that must be taken in a specific time frame to accomplish the goal. For example:

1. **CGC #1** Research Learning Leadership
- **WS Goal # 1**
    - Read the book
        - Action steps
        - Order the book online or go to the book store. Have it by 12/1/17.
        - Create reading schedule of 1 hour every evening from 5 PM-6 PM starting on 12/2/17.
        - Set aside one notebook for notes and research to be used when writing the white paper. Keep this with the book at all times.

Once you have all of your CGCs completed with WS goals and action steps, transfer the action steps to your calendar and keep yourself accountable to your timelines.

Have a mini-celebration every time you achieve one of your goals! Now, write a summary of your plan and keep it where you can see it and refer to it every day.

LEADERSHIP DEVELOPMENT PLAN SUMMARY

Vision Statement

_____
_____
_____
_____
_____
_____

Mission Statement

_____
_____
_____
_____
_____
_____

Critical Goal Categories (CGC's)

1) _____

2) _____

3) _____

4) _____

5) _____

6) _____

Chapter 10 - Do or Do Not. There is no Try. Yoda

You have just taken a monumental leap toward taking command of your ship and your success. Now I know some of this may seem tedious and even quite basic, but if you are not doing it, you are selling yourself short. This kind of discipline and planning is key to accomplishing what we want in our lives and careers. Each step and each piece of this process is connected to the one before and the one after—it is the scaffolding of a powerful web of skills, talent, knowledge, goals and actions that you are weaving to become an even better leader, and even better human.

Be a Leader that sets goals and accomplishes them, a Leader that gets things done, a Leader that produces results, a Leader that walks their talk, shares visions, challenges themselves and others, gives away their gifts, cares and genuinely connects to others.

This process is critical to strengthening, expanding and impacting our leadership influence and in building and weaving our webs with other human beings—connecting and learning and finding new and innovative ways to think, do and become. This is not just an exercise—it is a life-long tool—that is linked to everything in your web and drives accomplishment and success. This NEEDS to become a habit of thought!

 **GO FOR GOLD**

- Do or do not. There is no try. Are trying or doing? Doing requires action – planned action with specific goals that are achieved in a specific time frame. Keep yourself accountable to your plan every day.

- Remember your three 'i's. Keep them in front of you and review daily. What inspires you? Do more of it. How will you ignite it? Stick to your plan. What impact will you make? Take the actions necessary to actualize your plan and your vision.
- Be thoughtful and specific when writing your vison; mission, CCC's and WS Goals. Stay true to the plan.
- Who is in your web? How can you help them? How can they help you?

CHAPTER 11

THE SECRET SAUCE

> CLOWNING IS A TRICK TO GET LOVE CLOSE. I CAN HUG 99 PERCENT OF PEOPLE IN THE FIRST SECOND OF CONTACT IF I'M IN MY CLOWN CHARACTER. THE CLOWN ASSUMES YOUR HUMANITY. IT ASSUMES THAT, WHATEVER TRAUMA YOU'VE HAD, YOU CAN STILL LOVE YOURSELF.
>
> **PATCH ADAMS**

WHAT A PROFOUND QUOTE "whatever trauma you've had, you can still love yourself." If only more people realized this. As human beings, we go through all kinds trauma and drama in our lives and so often we internalize it as some sort of weakness, shortcoming or character flaw on our part. Truth be told, it just being human.

THE FOUR-LETTER WORD

What does this have to do with leadership? Well everything, really. At the very core of every great leader there is one thing that is unshakeable to them. And remember, we are talking about real leadership—not title, power, authority, etc.—those things are not leadership. They are part of it sometimes and sometimes not, but genuine leadership stems from something else. That something else is what I call the Secret Sauce of leadership.

You guessed it. Love.

Go back and look at your five core values. The exercise we did at the very beginning of the book. What are they? What is the ONE core value that you set apart from all the others that is your number one? The one that drives everything you do? Whatever it is—that is your love, your passion—your purpose by which the quality of your life is measured by you. The most important person in your life.

It's OK to say that. It's better than OK, it is imperative! If you are not the most important person in your life, then you are doing everyone else in your life a great disservice. Obviously, this is not about your ego—it is everything but that!

Love of self is where all authenticity starts. If you cannot love, like and respect yourself—with all your talents, warts, beauty, faults, brains, silliness and all the things (the good, bad and ugly) that make you, you—then how can you expect others to love, like and respect you?

This is the love story, my friends! It's not some romantic romp with another person—it's learning to love yourself no matter how many never wear red's you have heard or experienced in your life. You will always hear these things. It's what you DO with it that matters. It's always being present as your most authentic self, every day. It's being in each day with purpose, intention, focus and taking the action necessary to become your best self.

As Kouzes and Posner say, "the greatest leaders are the greatest learners", and learning about oneself—who we have been, who we are now—and who want to become is the greatest gift of leadership you can give yourself and all those you meet.

It is indeed a leadership love story.

The best part is—the longer we are on the journey, the older we get—the better the story becomes.

Everything in this book is about this simple, yet profound concept. It's about shedding all the STUFF that holds you back from being you. This is the foundation of leadership, confidence, emotional intelligence, empathy, selflessness, success, happiness and helping others.

Go take another look in the mirror. Go ahead. Right now. No one is looking but you. I won't tell. Who do you see? Do like them? Respect them? Love them? What do you need to do to start or increase all three with that person in the mirror? Write it down. Make a plan. Do.

Empathy & Compassion

As with emotional intelligence, empathy and compassion are big components in being an authentic leader. Even when tough love is the best approach—whether with yourself or with others—doing so with empathy and compassion is a much more effective and genuine way to help yourself and others.

Think about yourself at work or in a family situation that is emotionally charged, most likely a negative or stressful encounter (or one that could become negative), and how these things usually end. Are the outcomes the best they could be? Why or why not?

If they are not turning out in the best way possible for everyone, what can you do differently to have a positive impact on the outcomes?

Empathy and compassion will go a long way to making the outcomes better. This is not about emotion. It is about emotional intelligence. Empathy is listening first—not talking. Listening for understanding, perspective and how the other person or people feel about what is happening. It is not buying into the emotion, but rather connecting to the issue and how the other person feels about it and wanting to help them get to a better place with it.

Think about people you have known who are really good at this. They bring calm to highly charged situations; they are able to dial down emotion in others; they are able to deftly level the playing field and create opportunity for open discussion without making less of any one person or group of people. They lead. And they do it with empathy and compassion—a balance of right and left brain. They are leaders we enjoy working with and enjoy following.

And oh, by the way, they also know when to step aside and let others lead. The greatest leaders also make the greatest followers. You cannot have one without the other.

 **GO FOR GOLD**

- What is your ONE most important value? This is what guides you, your decisions, your thoughts and behavior. Mine is a four-letter word. What is yours?
- Are you listening, leading, living with empathy and compassion? If not, how can you? what can you do, what behavior can you adopt to use both to become a better leader of self and others?

CHAPTER 12

CORNERSTONES

> IF WE ARE TO GO FORWARD, WE MUST GO BACK AND REDISCOVER THOSE PRECIOUS VALUES—THAT ALL REALITY HINGES ON MORAL FOUNDATIONS AND THAT ALL REALITY HAS SPIRITUAL CONTROL.
>
> **MARTIN LUTHER KING, JR.**

TIME TO PAUSE AND REFLECT for a moment. Go back and review your strategic summary—your vision, values, principles, mission, critical goal categories, why smart goals and action steps.

Do you know where you are going? Do you know how you are going to get there? You have the tools. Now is the time to Captain your own ship. Write down every never wear red you can remember and flip all of those you cannot, you should not, you will never, and all the other limiting messages you have received—whether intended or not—and flip them around to I can, I will, I am.

THE FOUNDATION

Your foundation is built on a simple formula. It is the three 'i's.

Chapter 12 - Cornerstones

- inspire
- ignite
- impact

This is YOU to the power of three. Repeat after me:

i to the power of 3...i to the power of 3... i to the power of 3.

What is your inspiration? This is your passion, purpose and source of your power.

How will you ignite it? Make your plan. You need a step-by-step strategy to execute on your passion. You do as much for a vacation—why wouldn't you do this for your life?

Make an impact—the impact you want to have on your life and the lives of others. Take the action necessary every day to accomplish your goals and achieve your vision.

VALUE

A word about promises. Keep them. If you cannot keep them, don't make them. Simple.

Living a life of value is about a lot of things—many discussed in these pages. Keeping promises is a huge part of that, as are the four agreements as explained in the book, "The Four Agreements," by Don Miguel Ruiz. The author gives us 4 principles for living a life of value that are worth revisiting as we embark on our own journeys of success and happiness.

Here is a quick overview of The Four Agreements:

1. *Be impeccable with your word.*
2. *Don't take anything personally.*
3. *Don't make assumptions.*

4. Always do your best.

BE IMPECCABLE WITH YOUR WORD.

Speak with integrity. Say only what you mean. Avoid using words to speak against yourself or to gossip about others. Use the power of your word in the direction of truth and kindness.

Remember: Your opinion is nothing but your point of view—and not necessarily true. It reflects your beliefs and ego. We spread gossip and opinions so we can defend our point of view.

> "WHATEVER GAMES ARE PLAYED WITH US, WE MUST PLAY NO GAMES WITH OURSELVES."
>
> **RALPH WALDO EMERSON**

DON'T TAKE ANYTHING PERSONALLY.

This is a tough one for most of us. It's difficult to remember—especially in the moment, that nothing others do is because of you. What others say and do is a projection of their own reality, their own dream.

Refuse to take it personally, and you're free to act in accordance with your values—not theirs.

> "WHEN WE FEEL STUCK, GOING NOWHERE—EVEN STARTING TO SLIP BACKWARD—WE MAY ACTUALLY BE BACKING UP TO GET A RUNNING START."
>
> **DAN MILLMAN**

DON'T MAKE ASSUMPTIONS.

Find the courage to ask questions and to express what you really want. Communicate with others as clearly as you can to avoid misunderstandings, sadness, and drama. With just this one agreement, you can completely transform your life.

> "DO WHAT YOU FEEL IN YOUR HEART TO BE RIGHT—FOR YOU'LL BE CRITICIZED ANYWAY."
> **FRANKLIN D. ROOSEVELT**

ALWAYS DO YOUR BEST.

Your best is going to change from moment to moment; it will be different when you are healthy as opposed to sick. Under any circumstance, simply do your best, and you will avoid self-judgment, self-abuse, and regret.

Doing your best will bring out the best in others.

> "DO NOT FOLLOW WHERE THE PATH MAY LEAD. GO INSTEAD WHERE THERE IS NO PATH AND LEAVE A TRAIL."
> **RALPH WALDO EMERSON**

Practice.

Instead of trying to change another person, make an impact on someone you can really change: yourself.

If you have not yet read The Four Agreements, I encourage you to do so. It offers wisdom and clarity around living a life of value.

Gold Nuggets

Give it away – all of it

Do not be afraid to give away your gifts. That's why we have them. Once we figure out why we are here and start living in that space, our strength, our unique talents and our passion grow and develop exponentially. The only way to continue to become the best version of ourselves is to give it all away—all of it. And although it is not the reason we give our gifts away, a funny thing does happen when we do—the power of giving comes back to us ten-fold.

Trite but True – it's a journey

OK. We all know it's about the journey and not the destination. It's true, but having goals along the way is critical to success—so establishing small destinations to reach allows us to feel the sense of accomplishment we need to continue on to the next part of the trip. It spurs us on. Gives us confidence. And affirms our ability to achieve the goals we set out to meet. Celebrate every single one of them! This is what we so often forget to do once something is checked off the list, we immediately move on to the next. Stop for a moment! Celebrate the accomplishment! Congratulate yourself! Not too much, now, but at least for a moment—soak it in. Now—get off your laurels and get back to work (she said with a smile).

Up The Bar – wash, rinse, repeat

Every time you think you have done the very best you can—think again. How much better can you do it the next time? What lessons have you learned along the way and what will do with that knowledge? How can you become even more of who you want to be? Who can you help today? What impact—what imprint can you leave on the world in this very day to make it a better place?

Ask yourself these questions, and then wash, rinse, repeat.

Rock the Boat

As Jim Kouzes and Barry Posner would say, "challenge the process." Don't be numbed by the status quo. Look for ways to do things differently. If it ain't broke, break it. See if you can make it better. Just because a process, a pattern, a way of doing has always been done a certain way, doesn't mean it's the best way. Challenge yourself and others to think differently, act differently, approach issues and challenges differently—rock the boat! And see if you can do it without putting yourself (ego) in the picture. Do it for the simple reason to make a positive change and watch what happens.

Be A Legacy

There is one thing for sure in this life—it will end for each of us one day. This is not to be negative or sad; it's just a fact and part of living. As far as I know, we only get to live this life once, so we better make the best of it. One the ways we can do that is to think about what we want our legacy to be. How do you want to be remembered and thought of? What and who will you *inspire* in your lifetime? How will you *ignite* passion, purpose and power in others and the world in your lifetime? What actions, behavior and involvement will you engage in that will make an **impact** on the success and happiness of others in your lifetime? What is YOUR *i to the power of 3?* You are writing a bit of your legacy every day. Is it the legacy you want to leave?

No Limits

We put self-imposed limits on ourselves all the time—and we don't even realize it. Becoming more self-aware of this is critical. Otherwise, we stay stuck in the same old way of thinking about ourselves and our capabilities and potential. Many of these limitations come from others telling us who we are, should be, what we are capable of and what we are not. Push yourself to really question that self-talk whispering in your ear that you are not good-enough, smart enough, pretty or handsome enough, tough enough, the list is endless. Practice believing (even if you don't) that there are no limits to what you can do, accomplish, become, just for a moment, dream! The more you do this, the more the limits show themselves and then fade away. Really. Take off the shackles that are holding you down—there are no limits—only the ones you imagine.

Success

You possess more internal ability than you will ever use. The biggest obstacles you face are the limitations you place in your own mind. Individuals are goal seekers by nature and you are at your happiest when you are working toward the accomplishment of goals that are related to your major purpose in life. True success comes from identifying goals in all areas of life that are important to you, and organizing your time and energy so that all these areas are given priority.

Achievement

Achievement has little regard for age, nationality, gender or station in life.

It bestows itself upon those who dare to aim their sights at noble targets, who move forward even though the winds of opposition try to push them back, who realize their purpose is far greater than any obstacle that may appear to stand in their way.

How we lead our lives determines our future and the future of those around us. You have the unlimited potential to reach new heights for yourself and for others to create new products, new applications, new solutions, new organizations, new ideas and even a new and better world.

THE ART OF CHANGING YOURSELF

> "THE ART OF CHANGING YOURSELF REQUIRES THE SUBSTITUTING OF NEW HABITS FOR OLD. YOU MOLD YOUR CHARACTER AND YOUR FUTURE BY YOUR THOUGHTS AND ACTS. YOU CANNOT CLIMB UPHILL BY THINKING DOWNHILL THOUGHTS. IF YOUR WORLD IS GLOOMY AND HOPELESS, IT IS BECAUSE YOU ARE GLOOMY AND HOPELESS. YOU MUST CHANGE YOUR MIND TO CHANGE YOUR WORLD. MAKE YOURSELF DO WHAT NEEDS TO BE DONE. MAN ALONE, OF ALL THE CREATURES OF THIS EARTH, IS ARCHITECT OF HIS DESTINY.
>
> **"THE ART OF LIVING"**
> **WILFRED A. PETERSON**

> "FIGURE OUT WHAT YOU'RE GOOD AT AND START HELPING OTHER PEOPLE WITH IT; GIVE IT AWAY. PAY IT FORWARD. KARMA SORT OF WORKS BECAUSE PEOPLE ARE VERY

CONSISTENT. ON A LONG ENOUGH TIMESCALE, YOU WILL ATTRACT WHAT YOU PROJECT."

NAVAL RAVIKANT

BLESSINGS

You know all of those truisms we heard when we were growing up? Those old adages that told us to be cautious, not to risk too much, to believe (and prepare for) the worst that could happen? Ever wonder what life would look like if you flipped those statements around?

This Ronald Wallace poem offers the following...

"*Blessings occur.*
Some days I find myself putting my foot in the same stream twice;
leading a horse to water and making him drink.
I have a clue.
I can see the forest for the trees.
All around me people are making silk purses out of sows' ears,
getting blood from turnips, building Rome in a day.
There is a business like show business.
There is something new under the sun.
Some days misery no longer loves company; it puts itself out of its.
There is rest for the weary.
There is turning back.
There are guarantees.
I can be serious. I can mean that.
You can quite put your finger on it. Really.
Some days I know I am long for this world.

Chapter 12 - Cornerstones

I can go home again.
And when I go, I can take it with me."

What are you doing differently to become more of who you really are? What are your goals? What are you doing to achieve them? How will today be any different than a year from now? What are you doing to make a difference—for yourself, for your family, for your professional growth and success?

Set goals.

Take action.

Emerge as a Champion.

Do it.

Now.

Success is the continual achievement of your own predetermined goals, stabilized by balance and purified by belief.

"THE ONLY PERSON YOU ARE DESTINED TO BECOME IS THE PERSON YOU DECIDE TO BE."

RALPH WALDO EMERSON

 **GO FOR GOLD**

No matter your age or circumstance, you can change your life. It starts with self. Understanding you first and knowing that you are 100% responsible and accountable for yourself and your life. No one else. Success and happiness as you define it for yourself is not outside of you—it is inside of you.

External forces do not make or break you. Internal forces do. Once you recognize this, you are on your way to creating your life on your terms and in your time. It takes courage, grit, determination, passion and hard work to dig out your 0.2 mg of gold—but you can do it and the rewards are limitless. Go for your 0.2 mg of gold.

Emerge as a Champion.

Chapter 12 - Cornerstones

Thank you for walking along this Never Wear Red journey with me. It is indeed a leadership love story. We all have a story to tell and this is just part of mine. I hope you have found a few things to take away that will help you in your journey to emerge as the champion you already are and fully engage that 0.2 mg of gold in your heart and pay it forward.

Discover those never wear red obstacles in your life—put them out on the table. Disconnect them from your mind, body and soul and start overcoming them.

Find your **inspiration;**

ignite it with a solid plan;

make your **impact** on the world with your thoughts, actions, behavior and passion.

Embrace your red and your *i to the power of 3*.

With love,

Roxanne

P.S.

"Always Wear Red"

Resources

George Eliot

> "It is never too late to become what you might have been."
>
> **George Eliot**

Mary Ann Evans known by her pen name **George Eliot**, was an English novelist, poet, journalist, translator and one of the leading writers of the Victorian era.

> "What we think, we become."
>
> **Buddha**

Gautama Buddha

Gautama Buddha, also known as **Siddhārtha Gautama**, **Shakyamuni Buddha**,[note 3] or simply the **Buddha**, after the title of Buddha, was an ascetic (śramana) and sage,[3] on whose teachings Buddhism was founded.[web 2] He is believed to have lived and taught mostly in the eastern part of ancient India sometime between the sixth and fourth centuries BCE.

THEODORE MARTIN HESBURGH

Theodore Martin Hesburgh, CSC (May 25, 1917 – February 26, 2015), was a priest of the Congregation of Holy Cross, was president of the University of Notre Dame for 35 years. He is the namesake for TIAA-CREF's Hesburgh Award

"IN ORDER TO SUCCEED,
WE MUST FIRST BELIEVE THAT WE CAN."
NIKOS KAZANTZAKIS

NIKOS KAZANTZAKIS

18 February 1883 – 26 October 1957) was a Greek writer, celebrated for his novels, which include *Zorba the Greek* (published 1946 as *Life and Times of Alexis Zorbas*), Christ Recrucified (1948), Captain Michalis (1950, translated 'Freedom or Death), and The Last Temptation of Christ (1955). He also wrote plays, travel books, memoirs and philosophical essays such as The Saviors of God: Spiritual Exercises.

Universally recognized as a giant of modern Greek literature, Kazantzakis was nominated for the Nobel Prize in Literature in nine different years.[2]

His fame was further spread in the English speaking world by cinematic adaptations of *Zorba the Greek* (1964) and *The Last Temptation of Christ* (1988).

Strengths Finder 2.0 by Tom Rath (http://www.strengths-finder.com/home.aspx)

TOM RATH

Tom Rath (born 1975) is an American consultant on employee engagement, strengths, and well-being, and author. He is best known for his studies on strengths based leadership and wellbeing and synthesizing research findings in a series of bestselling books.[1][2] His books have sold more than 5 million copies and have been translated into sixteen languages.

THE HARTMAN COLOR CODE (HTTPS://WWW.COLORCODE.COM/)

- The **Color Code Personality Profile** also known as The Color Code or The People Code, created by Dr. Taylor Hartman, divides personalities into four colors: Red (motivated by power), Blue (motivated by intimacy), White (motivated by peace), and Yellow (motivated by fun). Although different groups of people have different demographics, the general breakdown suggests that Reds comprise 25% of the population; Blues 35%; Whites 20%; and Yellows 20%.[1] A 45-question test assesses one's color, based on whether you answer A, B, C, or D.

- DISC and VALUES Assessments. There are many different versions of the DISC assessment and VALUES- based assessments. It's a matter of which one you feel most comfortable with and if you will be working with a certified facilitator and/or coach. It is always my recommendation that you work with certified professionals on any kind of assessment to be sure you get the most out of the process.

- The LPI 360 – I use many different assessments, but I can say without hesitation that the Leadership Practices Inventory®

(LPI) by Jim Kouzes and Barry Posner (A Wiley Company) is by far the best 360-degree instrument I have ever used. Based on over 30 years of research and quantifiable results, this is a tool that can transform individual leadership as well as entire cultures of leaderships. The Leadership Challenge is a global campaign to liberate the leader in everyone. We believe that teams, businesses—and even the world—get better when ordinary people enable those around them to achieve extra-ordinary things. More information can be found at www.prolaureate.com; www.lpionline.com and www.theleadershipchallenge.com.

- There are many versions of Values Assessment—The Leadership Challenge workshop uses Value Cards and the one that we used in this book is from the women's leadership program, SOAR (Peer Exchange Network). SOAR is a one-of-a-kind professional development program for high-potential young women who have proven their readiness to advance within their organization. These young women are nominated by executives at their companies, they typically have 7-17 years of experience and they've demonstrated a willingness to take on new challenges and responsibilities.

MALCOM COHAN

Magic Happens - How to make a VISION Statement Video by Malcolm Cohan

Make a short video about your Vision - all the things you want - and your quest - the magical thing you came here to do.

I created VISION Statement in June 2006 to help people get

clarity about their lives - and since then thousands of people have made this magic journey.

Come join my Facebook group for everything you need to make a great Viz - Mac and PC software, tutorials and a great community of Visionaries to help you.

http://www.facebook.com/group.php?gid=5123202899

Join me in this magical process!

Producer Malcolm Cohan

SIMON O. SINEK

Simon O. Sinek (born October 9, 1973) is an author, speaker, and consultant who writes on leadership and management. He joined the RAND Corporation in 2010 as an adjunct staff member, where he advises on matters of military innovation and planning]. He is known for popularizing the concepts of "the golden circle" and to "Start With Why",[1][2][3] described by TED as "a simple but powerful model for inspirational leadership all starting with a golden circle and the question "Why?"". [4] Sinek's first TEDx Talk on "How Great Leaders Inspire Action" is the 3rd most viewed video on TED.com.[5][6] His 2009 book on the same subject, Start With Why: How Great Leaders Inspire Everyone to Take Action (2009) delves into what he says is a naturally occurring pattern, grounded in the biology of human decision-making, that explains why we are inspired by some people, leaders, messages and organizations over others. He has commented for The New York Times, Wall Street Journal, The Washington Post, Houston Chronicle, FastCompany, CMO Magazine, NPR, and BusinessWeek, and was a regular contributor to The Huffington Post, BrandWeek, IncBizNet

Charlie Chaplin

Sir Charles Spencer "Charlie" Chaplin, KBE (16 April 1889 – 25 December 1977) was an English comic actor, filmmaker, and composer who rose to fame during the era of silent film. Chaplin became a worldwide icon through his screen persona "the Tramp" and is considered one of the most important figures in the history of the film industry.[1] His career spanned more than 75 years, from childhood in the Victorian era until a year before his death in 1977, and encompassed both adulation and controversy.

The Cowardly LionThe Wizard of Oz

The **Cowardly Lion** is a character in the fictional Land of Oz created by American author L. Frank Baum.[1] He is an African Lion, but he speaks and interacts with humans.

Since lions are supposed to be "The Kings of Beasts," the Cowardly Lion believes that his fear makes him inadequate. He does not understand that courage means acting in the face of fear, which he does frequently. Only during the aftereffects of the Wizard's gift, when he is under the influence of an unknown liquid substance that the Wizard orders him to drink (perhaps gin) is he not filled with fear. He argues that the courage from the Wizard is only temporary, although he continues to do brave deeds while openly and embarrassedly fearful.

Sir Winston Churchill

Sir Winston Leonard Spencer-Churchill KG OM CH TD PC DL FRS RA (30 November 1874 – 24 January 1965) was a British statesman who was the Prime Minister of the United

Kingdom from 1940 to 1945 and again from 1951 to 1955. Churchill was also an officer in the British Army, a non-academic historian, a writer (as Winston S. Churchill), and an artist. He won the Nobel Prize in Literature in 1953 for his overall, lifetime body of work. In 1963, he was the first of only eight people to be made an honorary citizen of the United States.

RESOURCE ASSOCIATES CORPORATION, READING, PA.

RAC's focus is simple: to help people become better at what they have been trained to do by helping them develop to their fullest potential, so the organization can accomplish its goals and objectives. They provide Consultants and Coaches with the knowledge and the tools they need to align with organizations in order to create cultures where continuous improvement, high levels of achievement, and customer loyalty prevail.

THE LEADERSHIP CHALLENGE

Jim Kouzes and Barry Posner. TLC is a global campaign to liberate the leader in everyone. We believe that teams, businesses—and even the world—get better when ordinary people enable those around them to achieve extra-ordinary things. More information can be found at www.prolaureate.com; www.lpionline.com and www.theleadershipchallenge.com.

SOAR (PEER EXCHANGE NETWORK).

SOAR is a one-of-a-kind professional development program for high-potential young women who have proven their readiness to advance within their organization.

These young women are nominated by executives at their companies, they typically have 7-17 years of experience and they've demonstrated a willingness to take on new challenges and responsibilities. www.seejanesoar.com

RISING MEDIA LLC.

Rising Media, LLC does great things, simply. We are the proud parent company of our digital magazine for achieving multi-stage professionals: Project Heard and it's older sister: The Woman of Power Conference held annually in Cleveland, Ohio. Rising Media, LLC was founded by former TV news broadcaster, Raquel Eatmon who is the current CEO. Raquel has built a media empire on the principles of promise to our Services, Clients, Humanity, Partners, Staff/ Volunteers and Advisory Board.

OUR MISSION: We work through various channels with the intent of producing positive and high-performance related conversions in the human experience. To put it simply: We develop content and events to help build stronger leaders around the world. We do this through a trifecta approach. www.projectheard.com

MARGEAU'S "FREE TO BE" PROJECT

Founder, Gail Stumphauzer - empowering women and girls to embrace their value and self-worth.

THE HUFFINGTON POST

http://www.huffingtonpost.com/news/women-in-the-boardroom/

The Huffington Post is a left-leaning American online news aggregator and blog that has both localized and international editions founded by Arianna Huffington, Kenneth Lerer, Jonah Peretti, and briefly, Andrew Breitbart, featuring columnists.

DEEPAK CHOPRA

Deepak Chopra is an American author, public speaker, alternative medicine advocate, and a prominent figure in the New Age movement. Through his books and videos, he has become one of the best-known and wealthiest figures in alternative medicine.

HARLEY DAVIDSON

"Harley Davidson motorcycles have evolved into so much more than just a brand name since their early 1900 beginnings. Their humble American start laid the ground work for the reputation of hardworking [people] and original [brand that] the Harley Davidson motorcycle still has today. Motorcyclists embrace this originality and express it in an outlaw, subculture society that appeals to a lot of humanity.

RICHARD EYRE

Born in Barnstaple, Devon, England, Eyre was educated at Sherborne School, an independent school for boys in the market town of Sherborne in northwest Dorset in southwest England, followed by Peterhouse at the University of Cambridge.

Eyre became the first president of Rose Bruford College in July 2010.[1] He gives "President's Lectures" at this prestigious drama school; his 2012 talk was entitled "Directing Shakespeare for BBC Television".[2] He lives in Brook Green, West London.

Resources

Eleanor Roosevelt

Anna Eleanor Roosevelt (/ˈɛlɪnɔːr ˈroʊzəvɛlt/; October 11, 1884 – November 7, 1962) was an American politician, diplomat, and activist.[1] She was the longest-serving First Lady of the United States, having held the post from March 1933 to April 1945 during her husband President Franklin D. Roosevelt's four terms in office,[1] and served as United States Delegate to the United Nations General Assembly from 1945 to 1952.[2] [3] President Harry S. Truman later called her the "First Lady of the World" in tribute to her human rights achievements.

Frank Lloyd Wright

Frank Lloyd Wright (born **Frank Lincoln Wright**, June 8, 1867 – April 9, 1959) was an American architect, interior designer, writer, and educator, who designed more than 1,000 structures, 532 of which were completed. Wright believed in designing structures that were in harmony with humanity and its environment, a philosophy he called organic architecture. This philosophy was best exemplified by Fallingwater (1935), which has been called "the best all-time work of American architecture". [1] Wright was a leader of the Prairie School movement of architecture and developed the concept of the Usonian home, his unique vision for urban planning in the United States. His creative period spanned more than 70 years.

Marcus Aureluis

Marcus Aurelius (/ɔːˈriːliəs/; Latin: Marcus Aurelius Antoninus Augustus;[1][notes 1] 26 April 121 – 17 March 180 CE) was Roman Emperor from 161 to 180. He ruled with Lucius

Verus as co-emperor from 161 until Verus' death in 169. Marcus Aurelius was the last of the so-called Five Good Emperors. He was a practitioner of Stoicism, and his untitled writing, commonly known as the Meditations, is the most significant source of the modern understanding of ancient Stoic philosophy.

KAREN RAVN

Karen Ravn is a published author. A published credit of Karen Ravn is Friendship saves the day (Storybook friends).

BARUCH SPINOZA

Baruch Spinoza (/bəˈruːk spɪˈnoʊzə/;[6] Dutch: [baːˈrux spɪˈnoːzaː]; born Benedito de Espinosa, Portuguese: [bɨniˈðitu ðɨ ʃpiˈnɔzɨ]; 24 November 1632 – 21 February 1677, later Benedict de Spinoza) was a Dutch philosopher of Sephardi/Portuguese origin.[5] By laying the groundwork for the 18th-century Enlightenment[7] and modern biblical criticism,[8] including modern conceptions of the self and the universe,[9] he came to be considered one of the great rationalists of 17th-century philosophy.

MARIANNE WILLIAMSON

Marianne Deborah Williamson (born July 8, 1952)[2] is an American spiritual teacher, author and lecturer. She has published eleven books, including four New York Times number one bestsellers. She is the founder of Project Angel Food, a meals-on-wheels program that serves homebound people with AIDS in the Los Angeles area, and the co-founder of The Peace Alliance, a grassroots campaign supporting legislation to establish a United States Department of Peace. She serves on the Board of Directors of the RESULTS organization, which works to end poverty in the United States and around the world. Williamson is also behind Sister Giant, a series of seminars and teaching sessions that provides women with the information and tools needed to be political candidates. Through these seminars,[3] she encourages women to run for office and align their politics with their spiritual values.

BRIAN TRACY

Brian Tracy (born 5 January 1944)[2] is a Canadian-born American motivational public speaker and self-development author.[3][4][5] He is the author of over 70 books that have been translated into dozens of languages.[6] His popular books are Earn What You're Really Worth,[7] Eat That Frog!,[8] and The Psychology of Achievement.[9] As an author, he has been largely collected by libraries worldwide.[10] He is married and has four children. www.briantracy.com.

CONSCIOUS LEADERSHIP GROUP (CLG)

Founded by Jim Dethmer and Diana Chapman, The Conscious Leadership Group (CLG) brings to the world a radically new conversation about leadership, consciousness, self-awareness and commitment through coaching, consulting, forums, tools, and speaking. CLG's leadership model is based on Jim and Diana's decades of experience and practice coaching, consulting, facilitating and speaking to CEOs, executive teams, leaders, YPO forums and organizations.

Kaley Warner Klemp

Kaley Warner Klemp is an engaging, highly sought after speaker, certified YPO Forum Facilitator, and transformational executive coach. She advises senior executives on how to uncover and address core challenges, provides them with proven tools and methods to reach new heights, and uses her years of experience to guide leaders towards achieving their goals. Additionally, she supports high performing teams using the Conscious Leadership practices to help high performing teams create a culture of authenticity and superior results.

Dwight D. Eisenhower

Dwight David "Ike" Eisenhower was the 34th President of the United States from 1953 until 1961. He was a five-star general in the United States Army during World War II and served as Supreme Commander of the Allied Expeditionary Forces in Europe.

David Bowie

David Robert Jones (8 January 1947 – 10 January 2016), known professionally as **David Bowie** (/ˈboʊi/),[2] was an English singer, songwriter and actor. He was a figure in _popular music_ for over five decades, regarded by critics and musicians as an innovator, particularly for his work in the 1970s. His career was marked by reinvention and visual presentation, his music and stagecraft significantly influencing popular music. During his lifetime, his record sales, estimated at 140 million worldwide, made him one of the _world's best-selling music artists_. In the UK, he was awarded nine platinum album certifications, eleven gold and eight silver, releasing _eleven number-one albums_. In the US, he received five platinum and seven gold certifications. He was inducted into the _Rock and Roll Hall of Fame_ in 1996.

JACK CANFIELD

Jack Canfield (born August 19, 1944[1][2]) is an American author, motivational speaker,[3] seminar leader, corporate trainer, and entrepreneur.[4]:453 He is the co-author of the Chicken Soup for the Soul series, which has more than 250 titles and 500 million copies in print in over 40 languages.[3][5] In 2005 Canfield co-authored with Janet Switzer The Success Principles: How to Get From Where You Are to Where You Want to Be

HAROLD GENEEN

Harold "Hal" Sydney **Geneen** (January 22, 1910 – November 21, 1997), was an American businessman most famous for serving as president of the ITT Corporation.

JOHN QUINCY ADAMS

John Quincy Adams was an American statesman who served as the sixth President of the United States from 1825 to 1829. He also served as a diplomat, a Senator and member of the House of Representatives.

PRESIDENT THEODORE ROOSEVELT

Theodore Roosevelt Jr. was an American statesman, author, explorer, soldier, naturalist, and reformer who served as the 26th President of the United States from 1901 to 1909

WILLIAM JAMES

William James (January 11, 1842 – August 26, 1910) was an American philosopher and psychologist who was also trained as a physician. The first educator to offer a psychology course in the United States,[3] James was one of the leading thinkers of the late nineteenth century and is believed by many to be one of the most influential philosophers the United States has ever produced, while others have labelled him the "Father of American psychology"

STEPHEN COVEY

Stephen Richards Covey (October 24, 1932 – July 16, 2012) was an American educator, author, businessman, and keynote speaker. His most popular book was The 7 Habits of Highly Effective People. His other books include First Things First, Principle-Centered Leadership, The 7 Habits of Highly Effective Families, The 8th Habit, and The Leader In Me — How Schools and Parents Around the World Are Inspiring Greatness, One Child at a Time. He was a professor at the Jon M. Huntsman School of Business at Utah State University at the time of his death.

JAMES TAYLOR

James Vernon Taylor (born March 12, 1948) is an American singer-songwriter and guitarist. A five-time Grammy Award winner, he was inducted into the Rock and Roll Hall of Fame in 2000.[2] He is one of the best-selling artists of all time, having sold more than 100 million records worldwide

CAROL KING

Carole King (born **Carol Joan Klein**, February 9, 1942) is

Resources

an American composer and singer-songwriter.[2] She is the most successful female songwriter of the latter 20th century, having written or co-written 118 pop hits on the Billboard Hot 100 between 1955 and 1999.[3] King also wrote 61 hits that charted in the UK,[4] making her the most successful female songwriter on the UK singles charts between 1952 and 2005

TALENTSMART®

TalentSmart®, TalentSmart is the world's premier provider of emotional intelligence (EQ). More than 75% of the Fortune 500 companies rely on our products and services. All of our cutting-edge assessments are easy to use, based on rigorous research, and include our proprietary e-learning and Goal-Tracking System™. Our training programs and coaching services ensure new skills are applied immediately. Our #1 best-selling, award-winning book Emotional Intelligence 2.0 is a groundbreaking addition to the application of EQ in the workplace.

MADELEINE ALBRIGHT

Madeleine Jana Korbel Albright[1] (born **Marie Jana Korbelová**; May 15, 1937)[2][3] is an American politician and diplomat. She is the first woman to have become the United States Secretary of State. She was nominated by U.S. President Bill Clinton on December 5, 1996, and was unanimously confirmed by a U.S. Senate vote of 99–0. She was sworn in on January 23, 1997.

ED MUZIO, PRESIDENT AND CEO OF GROUP HARMONICS

Founded by Ed Muzio in 2004, Group Harmonics has helped countless organizations produce higher output, lower stress, and sustainable growth. Originally educated as an engineer from Cornell University, Ed uses an analytical, research-based approach for solving common workplace challenges. you seek.

MARIO ANDRETTI

Mario Gabriele Andretti (born February 28, 1940) is an Italian American former racing driver, one of the most successful Americans in the history of the sport. He is one of only two drivers to have won races in Formula One, IndyCar, World Sportscar Championship and NASCAR (the other being Dan Gurney). He also won races in midget cars, and sprint cars. During his career, Andretti won the 1978 Formula One World Championship, four IndyCar titles (three under USAC-sanctioning, one under CART), and IROC VI. To date, he remains the only driver ever to win the Indianapolis 500 (1969), Daytona 500 (1967) and the Formula One World Championship, and, along with Juan Pablo Montoya, the only driver to have won a race in the NASCARSprint Cup Series, Formula One, and an Indianapolis 500. No American has won a Formula One race since Andretti's victory at the 1978 Dutch Grand Prix. [1] Andretti had 109 career wins on major circuits.

SHAWN ACHOR

Shawn Achor (born 1978)[1] is an American happiness researcher, author, and speaker known for his advocacy of positive psychology.[2] He authored The Happiness Advantage[3] and founded GoodThink,Inc.[4] His TEDxBloomington talk "The Happy Secret to Better Work"[5] is one of the 20-most viewed TED talks.

PATCH ADAMS

Hunter Doherty "Patch" Adams (born May 28, 1945) is an American physician, comedian, social activist, clown, and author. He founded the Gesundheit! Institute in 1971. Each year he organizes a group of volunteers from around the world to travel to various countries where they dress as clowns in an effort to bring humor to orphans, patients, and other people.

DON MIGUEL RUIZ.

Don Miguel Ángel Ruiz, better known as Don Miguel Ruiz, is a Mexican author of Toltec spiritualist and neoshamanistic texts. His work is part of the New Age movement that focuses on ancient teachings as a means to achieve spiritual enlightenment.

RALPH WALDO EMERSON

Apr 2, 2014 - **Ralph Waldo Emerson** was **born** on May 25, 1803, in Boston, Massachusetts. In 1821, he took over as director of his brother's school for girls. In 1823, he wrote the poem "Good-Bye." In 1832, he became a Transcendentalist, leading to the later essays "Self-Reliance" and "The American Scholar."

DAN MILLMAN

Daniel Jay Millman is an American author and lecturer in the personal development field. Wikipedia

Born: February 22, 1946 (age 70), Los Angeles, CA

Spouse: Joy Millman

Education: University of California, Berkeley

Movies: Peaceful Warrior

WILFRED A. PETERSON

Wilferd Arlan Peterson (1900–1995) was an American author who wrote for This Week magazine (a national Sunday supplement in newspapers) for many years. For twenty-five years, he wrote a monthly column for Science of Mind magazine. He published nine books starting in 1949 with The Art of Getting Along: Inspiration for Triumphant Daily Living."

NAVAL RAVIKANT

Naval Ravikant is the CEO and a co-founder of AngelList. He previously co-founded Epinions (which went public as part of Shopping.com) and Vast.com. He is an active Angel investor, and have invested in dozens of companies, including Twitter, Uber, Yammer, Stack Overflow and Wanelo.

RONALD WALLACE

Ronald Wallace is an American poet, and Felix Pollak Professor of Poetry & Halls-Bascom Professor of English at the University of Wisconsin–Madison.

CPSIA information can be obtained
at www.ICGtesting.com
Printed in the USA
FFOW02n2207100218
44939156-45184FF